Tim Challies has drawn from the warmhearted expressions of saints who have gone before us and added thoughtful reflections of his own. The result, *Pilgrim Prayers*, will provide fresh fuel for the fire of your devotion to the Lord.

—Nancy DeMoss Wolgemuth, author; Bible teacher; founder, Revive Our Hearts

When I first began investigating the Bible as an atheist, I simply wanted to know whether Christianity is true. I discovered it is both true and good, factual and beautiful. In *Pilgrim Prayers*, Tim Challies gives the church a moving reminder of Christianity's incredible power through inspiring poetry. This book will change the way you rejoice in God's grace in periods of plenty and trust in his provision in seasons of suffering. Let *Pilgrim Prayers* deepen your devotional life as it helps you explore the rich, beautiful, and creative history of Christian poetry.

—J. Warner Wallace, *Dateline*-featured cold-case detective; senior fellow, Colson Center for Christian Worldview; adjunct professor of apologetics, Talbot School of Theology (Biola Univ.); author, *The Truth in True Crime: What Investigating Death Teaches Us about the Meaning of Life*

Tim Challies is a treasure hunter. He has rummaged through the attic of Christian history, he has rediscovered priceless prayers written as poetry, he has dusted them off, and he has now brought them back out for use today. We are surrounded by a great cloud of witnesses—men and women who ran the race faithfully through prayer—and with Tim as a guide to deeper devotion to our Lord, we now can join our hearts to theirs, echoing their praises and petitions, giving glory to the same God who saves and sanctifies his people.

—Trevin Wax, vice president of resources and marketing, North American Mission Board; visiting professor, Cedarville University; author, *The Thrill of Orthodoxy*; *Rethink Your Self*; and the devotional prayer trilogy *Psalms in 30 Days*, *Life of Jesus in 30 Days*, *Letters of Paul in 30 Days*

pilgrim prayers

pilgrim prayers

devotional poems that awaken your heart to the goodness, greatness, and glory of god

TIM CHALLIES

ZONDERVAN REFLECTIVE

Pilgrim Prayers

Published in Grand Rapids, Michigan, by Zondervan. Zondervan is a registered trademark of The Zondervan Corporation, L.L.C., a wholly owned subsidiary of HarperCollins Christian Publishing, Inc.

Requests for information should be addressed to customercare@harpercollins.com.

Zondervan titles may be purchased in bulk for educational, business, fundraising, or sales promotional use. For information, please email SpecialMarkets@Zondervan.com.

ISBN 978-0-310-16642-9 (audio)

Library of Congress Cataloging-in-Publication Data

Names: Challies, Tim, 1976- author.
Title: Pilgrim prayers : devotional poems that awaken your heart to the goodness, greatness, and glory of God / Tim Challies.
Description: Grand Rapids, Michigan : Zondervan, [2024] | Includes index.
Identifiers: LCCN 2024011402 (print) | LCCN 2024011403 (ebook) | ISBN 9780310166405 (hardcover) | ISBN 9780310166412 (ebook)
Subjects: LCSH: Devotional exercises. | Spiritual life—Christianity. | Prayers. | BISAC: RELIGION / Christian Living / Devotional | RELIGION / Christian Rituals & Practice / Worship & Liturgy
Classification: LCC BV4801 .C44 2024 (print) | LCC BV4801 (ebook) | DDC 242/.8—dc23/eng/20240516
LC record available at https://lccn.loc.gov/2024011402
LC ebook record available at https://lccn.loc.gov/2024011403

Published in association with the literary agency of Wolgemuth & Wilson.

Cover design: Gearbox Studio
Cover photo: © Luke Gram / Stocksy
Interior design: Sara Colley

Printed in the United States of America

24 25 26 27 28 LBC 5 4 3 2 1

This book is dedicated to the memory of my friend David van Wingerden.

Life's labor done, as sinks the clay,
Light from its load the spirit flies,
While heaven and earth combine to say,
"How blest the righteous when he dies!"

contents

prayers

introduction

There was a time, and it was not so very long ago, when Christians valued poetry. There were entire ages when poetry was among the major forms of communication and when both reading and writing it was a common element of Christian spirituality. Thousands of Christians wrote devotional poems to express their praise to God or offer their prayers to him in poetic form. Thousands more Christians read these poems and benefited from them. Today, though, poetry has become an afterthought among most Christians. Few people write it and few people are aware of the vast treasuries that our forebears have bequeathed to us.

I discovered devotional poetry several years ago when I downloaded an app that promised to help me improve my memory. The app worked, and soon enough I had a number of wonderful poems available for instant recall. Again and again I recited these poems to myself until they were ingrained in my mind and heart. Little did I know how much I would rely on them when the Lord called me to endure a time of great suffering and sorrow. Those poems gave me words to express my griefs, truths to comfort my distress, and petitions to lift to the Lord. I learned to borrow the words of these poets, to make their words the expression of my heart, and to lift their words to the Lord as prayers.

Since then, I have spent many hours combing through the endless volumes of poetry written in years gone by. The most accessible poems I've found were written in the mid- to late-1800s, though there are some treasures from the 1700s as well. By the time we get all the way back to the 1600s and earlier, there are still many excellent works, but they are often a little more difficult to read and absorb because of their antiquated language.[1]

For this volume, I have collected fifty poems that are prayers to God—poems that are meant to help you pray. Some are meant to be prayed in the morning and some in the evening; some are confessions of sin and some are expressions of worship; some plead God's help in times of temptation and some plead his comfort in times of suffering; some look to God's great deeds in the past while some look to the great deeds God has promised to do in the future. But all

1. There were also some good poems written in the 1900s, and there are some good ones still being written today. Copyright issues begin to intrude, however, so I have not included any poems written within the past one hundred years.

are directed from the reader to the Lord—prayers that are written in the form of poems.

I have supplemented each one with a brief devotional, a couple of appropriate Bible verses, and a question or two of application. I have also added occasional notes to help you grow in your ability to read poetry and to enhance your love for it. I have slightly adapted some poems from the first person plural to the first person singular (from "we, us" to "I, me") to make them just a little bit easier to pray.

It is my hope and my confidence that these poems will serve you as well as they have served me—that you come to treasure them as you pray them as the expression of your own heart. To that end, perhaps it is fitting that we should turn first to a poem that can teach us about prayer. What is prayer? Why should you pray? And how can you grow in your desire and ability to pray? James Montgomery would like to teach you. Why don't you read the poem, then pause to make the words of the final stanza the prayer of your own heart.

Prayer is the soul's sincere desire,
Unuttered or expressed;
The motion of a hidden fire,
That trembles in the breast.

Prayer is the burden of a sigh,
The falling of a tear;

The upward glancing of an eye,
When none but God is near.

Prayer is the simplest form of speech
That infant lips can try;
Prayer, the sublimest strains that reach
The Majesty on high.

Prayer is the Christian's vital breath,
The Christian's native air;
His watchword at the gates of death—
He enters heaven with prayer.

Prayer is the contrite sinner's voice,
Returning from his ways;
While angels in their songs rejoice
And cry, "Behold, he prays!"

The saints in prayer appear as one,
In word, in deed, and mind;
While with the Father and the Son,
Sweet fellowship they find.

No prayer is made by man alone
The Holy Spirit pleads;
And Jesus, on th' eternal throne
For sinners intercedes.

O Thou! by Whom we come to God,
The Life, the Truth, the Way;
The path of prayer Thyself hast trod:
Lord, teach me how to pray.

May God answer that prayer through the pages of this book and the poetic prayers it contains.

reading and understanding poetry

Poetry is not prose. Prose is writing in its most common and familiar form. It is written in sentences and paragraphs and does not rely on meter or rhyme. Though it can still be rich and beautiful, it tends to express ideas plainly and functionally, without depending upon imagery and allusion. The words you are reading right now are prose.

Poetry, on the other hand, is written in lines and stanzas and typically has some pattern of meter and rhyme in which each line follows a familiar rhythm and the final syllable of a line may rhyme with one or more others. In this collection, at least, each of the poems has an identifiable meter and a distinct rhyme scheme. I have deliberately chosen poems that are relatively simple in both content and form. Poems also tend to rely on imagery and allusion so that instead of providing plain expressions of truth, they paint pictures with words.

And through their use of all of these techniques, poems tend to evoke emotion in a way prose does not. That makes poetry especially powerful. The best poetry uses words to engage our minds and the poetic form to engage our hearts.

Many wonder what the difference is between poems and hymns. The answer is not much. Hymns are essentially poems set to music. Many of the great hymns of the Christian faith were written first as poems and only later adapted for singing. In this collection, I have included a few lesser-known hymns but generally avoided the ones that are more familiar.

Here are a few tips on learning to read and enjoy poetry:

- Poetry is at its best when read aloud. When that is not possible, read it with your mind engaged *as if* you were reading it aloud.
- Try to immediately identify the meter and the rhyme scheme. Read with the meter in mind, but don't overdo it so it becomes choppy like a marching drum. Read it with the rhyme scheme in mind, but with a kind of subtlety so you are not overemphasizing the final syllable of the lines.
- Read the poem a first time to look for meter and rhyme and to discover any recurring imagery the author is using to tie the poem together.
- Read the poem a second time to better express your understanding of its meter, rhyme, and purpose.

- Read it a third time to focus more on the words and ideas and to understand how you might pray it to the Lord.
- Return to your favorites often because the more you read them, the more you'll understand them and the more you'll be able to make them the expression of your heart. Even consider memorizing the ones that prove important to you.

When you learn to read poetry, you'll find that there are vast stores of it awaiting you and many treasures to bless your heart, feed your mind, and help you live for the glory of God.

how to use this book

This book is meant to help you pray, to give you fresh ways to express yourself to the Lord in your prayers. It is a collection of prayers set to poetry. The majority of the poems are written from a personal perspective and use words such as "I" and "me." A few are written from a corporate perspective and use words such as "we" and "us." But all are directed from the reader to God as expressions of adoration, confession, thanksgiving, or supplication. I have created a title for each that summarizes the kind of prayer it is—"A Prayer of Confidence in God," "A Prayer of Confession," "A Prayer to Begin the Morning," and so on.

To make the best use of this book, I recommend reading the title of the poem, then the brief devotional that accompanies it. This will set your context. Then read the poem quickly once or twice to find the meter and rhyme and to gain a brief understanding of its content. Having done this, simply read the poem as a prayer—allow the poet to give you words to speak to the Lord. This may feel a little forced at first, as is often the case when reading prayers, but it will soon become natural and meaningful. If you would like to go a little bit deeper, I have included a couple of Bible verses related to each prayer and a couple of questions of personal application.

You can read one poem a day, you can read one in the morning and one in the evening, or you can read them all at once. Regardless, I recommend you return to them often because you will find that as you pray them again and again, they will begin to better express the desires of your heart.

prayers

a prayer of adoration for God's holiness

Holy, Holy, Holy Lord:
James Montgomery

In the English language we amplify or elevate a description by preceding it with words such as "very" or "extremely" or "exceedingly." This is how we distinguish between a man who is tall, a man who is unusually tall, and a man who is exceptionally tall. The Hebrew language, though, elevates words by repeating them. Thus a man who is exceptionally tall might be a "tall, tall man." The Bible often describes God's attributes, but there is only one attribute that is given a threefold repetition. God is good but is never described as good, good, good. God is just but is never described at just, just, just. Only his holiness is elevated to the third degree, only his holiness so defines him that it must be repeated three times over. He is not merely holy or holy, holy. He is holy, holy, holy. And because he is so very, extremely, exceedingly holy, he is worthy of our praise, our worship, our most earnest devotion. And so we worship this holy God, just as creation did when God established it, just as God's people do today as they rejoice in their salvation, and just as all of heaven and earth will do on the day when Christ returns.

observe

Observe how the poet gives words for you to express your worship and your wonder to God. Note also the progression of the poem from time past to time present to time future.

pray

Holy, Holy, Holy Lord,
God of Hosts! when heaven and earth,
Out of darkness at Thy word,
Issued into glorious birth,
All Thy works before Thee stood,
And Thine eye beheld them good,
While they sang with sweet accord,

Holy, Holy, Holy Lord!

Holy, Holy, Holy! Thee,
One Jehovah evermore,
Father, Son, and Spirit! we,
Dust and ashes, would adore;
Lightly by the world esteem'd,
From that world by Thee redeem'd,
Sing we here with glad accord,
Holy, Holy, Holy Lord!

Holy, Holy, Holy! All
Heaven's triumphant choirs shall sing,
When the ransom'd nations fall
At the footstool of their King:
Then shall saints and seraphim,
Hearts and voices swell one hymn,
Round the Throne with full accord,
Holy, Holy, Holy Lord!

—James Montgomery, "Holy, Holy, Holy Lord"

reflect

Isaiah 6:1–7; Revelation 5:1–14.

apply

How often do you pause to ponder God's holiness? How might your Christian life be different if you pondered it more often and with greater deliberateness?

a prayer to begin the morning

Hymn for the Morning: Thomas Flatman

God created us as finite and limited creatures. It is no bug in our system and no flaw in our design that we are dependent upon rest. We cannot function without breaks; we cannot long survive without sleep. And having slept through the darkness of night, we begin each new morning with a fresh start, a fresh opportunity to praise God, to serve him, and to depend upon his grace. Each day we need to not only open our eyes and rouse our bodies but also awaken our souls to the wonder of God's work of creation and the wonder of his work of redemption. We need to awaken our souls to ponder the character of the God who made us, saved us, and promised to bring us safely home to heaven. We need to awaken our souls to consider the gospel and to preach its glorious wonders to ourselves. "Awake, my soul!" we cry as we begin a new day. "Awake!"

observe

The first two lines end with the words "eyes" and "faculties." This is an accepted poetic form known as a half rhyme, in which the final consonants ("s") have the same sound but the vowels do not ("e" and "ies"). It is often used when the alternative would either not rhyme or rhyme in a way that was both expected and clichéd. Note also the half rhyme in the final stanza. When you come to a half rhyme as in "eyes" and "faculties," pronounce the latter as you normally would without trying to make it fully rhyme with "eyes"—"FAC-ul-teez" rather than "FAC-ul-teyes."

pray

Awake, my soul! awake, mine eyes!
Awake, my drowsy faculties;
Awake, and see the new-born light,
Spring from the darksome womb of night!

Look up and see the unwearied sun,
Already has his race begun.

The pretty lark is mounted high,
And sings her matins[1] in the sky.

Arise, my soul, and thou, my voice
In songs of praise early rejoice!
O great Creator! heav'nly King!
Thy praises let me ever sing!

Thy power has made, Thy goodness kept
This fenceless[2] body while I slept;
Yet one day more has given me
From all the powers of darkness free.

Oh! keep my heart from sin secure,
My life unblameable and pure;
That when the last of days shall come,
Cheerful and fearless I may wait my doom.

—Thomas Flatman, "Hymn for the Morning"

reflect

Psalm 57:8–10; Lamentations 3:22–24.

---

1. Morning prayer.
2. Defenseless.

apply

What habits or routines awaken your soul in the morning with praise and thanks to God? How disciplined are you in these practices? What habits or routines do you hold to even though they keep your soul dull and listless? What might God be calling you to do about these?

a prayer of praise to Christ

The Lamb of God: Christopher Newman Hall

The Bible describes Jesus as "the Lamb of God" (John 1:29). This is a reference back to Old Testament worship services in which God's people were to show their submission to him by offering an unblemished lamb as a sacrifice. Though they may not have understood it at the time, these sacrifices pointed forward to a final sacrifice—one final sacrifice that would render the entire system obsolete and unnecessary. For in that final sacrifice they would come to learn that all of those lambs had simply been leading toward Jesus Christ, the morally unblemished God-man who would willingly give up his life to permanently reconcile God and man. And that Lamb would be resurrected and exalted and declared worthy "to receive power and wealth and wisdom and might and honor and glory and blessing!" (Rev. 5:12). Who but God could create and fulfill a plan like this?

observe

Note the reference in the third stanza to being "fit" for Christ's home of rest. As you read and pray the poem, consider how your growth in the gospel in this life, especially through suffering and prayer, makes you fit for the life to come.

pray

O Lamb of God! that on the cross,
Didst suffer to atone my loss,
Give ear unto a sinner's plea,
Have mercy, Lamb of God! on me.

There's room within Thy wounded side;
For all transgressors Thou hast died;
Pardon for all hast Thou unfurled
Whose blood was shed for all the world.

O Lamb of God! grant me Thy peace,
From sin and sorrow send release,

And fit me for Thy home of rest,
To be with Thee for ever blest:

There may I join the ransomed throng,
And swell the everlasting song—
"Worthy the Lamb who once was slain,
Worthy for evermore to reign!"

—Christopher Newman Hall, "The Lamb of God"[1]

reflect

Isaiah 53:7; Revelation 5:6–14.

apply

Have you turned to Christ in repentance and faith? Can you say that the Lamb of God suffered to atone *your* loss? If not, would you consider doing so right now? For as the poet says to Jesus, "For *all* transgressors Thou hast died."

1. Adapted from plural to singular.

a prayer for strength and perseverance

I Pray for Strength: William Edward Biederwolf

The Christian life is not a life of ease. To the contrary, Jesus told his followers that to follow him they would first need to deny themselves and take up a cross. In that place and time, a cross represented suffering, humiliation, and death. And in that way he warned his followers that there would be a cost to following him. They would need to deny their natural desires to be loved and honored by others, their natural disposition toward a serene and untroubled life. Since then, every Christian has had to count the cost, consider how to suffer for his sake, and judge whether the price was worth it. Every Christian has had to rely upon God for his strengthening and sustaining grace while enduring a lifetime of trials, sorrows, and even persecutions. And such Christians have inevitably found that what they need, God is pleased to supply.

observe

The first and last stanzas parallel a request to God for strength to bear the burdens of life. The three stanzas between ask God to provide strength for specific purposes—to run dutifully, to wait submissively, and to live nobly. The rhyme pattern in this poem is a little more complex than some, but read carefully and you will find it.

pray

I pray for strength, O God!
To bear all loads that on my shoulders press
Of Thy directing or Thy chastening rod,
Lest from their growing stress
My spirit sink in utter helplessness.

I pray for strength to run
In duty's narrowest paths, nor turn aside
In broader ways that glow in pleasure's sun,
Lest I grow satisfied,

Where Thou from me Thy smiling face
    must hide.

I pray for strength to wait
Submissively when I cannot see my way,
Or if my feet would haste, some close-barred gate
Bids my hot zeal delay,
Or to some by-path turns their steps astray.

I pray for strength to live
To all life's noble ends, prompt, just and true;
Myself, my service, unto all give,
And, giving, yet renew
My store for bounty of life's journey through.

I pray, O God, for strength,
When, as life's love and labors find surcease,[1]
Cares, crosses, burdens to lay down at length,
And so, with joy's increase,
To die, if not in triumph—in Thy peace.

—William Edward Biederwolf, "I Pray for Strength"[2]

---

1. Cessation and relief.

2. This poem is found in William Edward Biederwolf, *How Can God Answer Prayer? Being an Exhaustive Treatise on the Nature, Conditions, and Difficulties of Prayer* (Chicago: Winona Publishing Co., 1906), 33.

reflect

Matthew 16:24; 2 Timothy 2:8–13.

apply

The poet prays for strength to face suffering, temptations, and uncertainty and to put on godly character and finish his life well. At this time in your life, where do you most feel the need for divine strength? Are you diligent in pleading with God for it?

a prayer to prepare the heart to pray

The Preparation of the Heart: James Montgomery

Prayer is one of the great privileges, great duties, and great delights of every Christian. Having been saved by God and adopted into his family, we now have the right to speak to him. And we can have confidence that he not only hears our prayers but also responds to them. So we pray to the Father, through the Spirit, by the Son—by the work of the Son in which he has redeemed us. Yet every Christian soon learns that prayer can be difficult at times. It can be difficult to know how to pray and what to pray. And it can be difficult to bring our hearts into a posture of confident, reverent submission in which we present our praises, confessions, and petitions before the Lord. For this reason it is often wise to begin our prayers with humility by simply asking God to help us to pray.

observe

Observe the specific requests the poet asks of God beginning in the third stanza: truth, humility, godly sorrow, a strong desire to hear God's voice, and so on.

pray

Lord, teach me how to pray aright,
With reverence and with fear;
Though dust and ashes in Thy sight,
I may, I must draw near.

I perish if I cease from prayer;
Oh! grant me power to pray;
And when to meet Thee I prepare,
Lord, meet me by the way.

Burden'd with guilt, convinced of sin,
In weakness, want, and woe

Fightings without, and fears within,
Lord, whither[1] shall I go?

God of all grace, I bring to Thee
A broken, contrite heart;
Give, what Thine eye delights to see,
Truth in the inward part.

Give deep humility; the sense
Of godly sorrow give;
A strong, desiring confidence
To hear Thy voice and live;—

Faith in the only Sacrifice
That can for sin atone;
To cast my love, to fix my eyes
On Christ, on Christ alone;—

Patience to watch, and wait, and weep,
Though mercy long delay;
Courage, my fainting soul to keep,
And trust Thee though Thou slay.

Give these, and then Thy will be done;
Thus, strenghen'd with all might,

1. Where else.

I, through Thy Spirit and Thy Son,
Shall pray, and pray aright.

—James Montgomery, "The Preparation of the Heart"[2]

reflect

Philippians 4:6; Hebrews 4:16.

apply

Though prayer is a privilege, duty, and delight, and though the Bible promises that God is eager and willing to hear our prayers, many Christians still struggle to pray. Are you comfortable with your current practice of prayer? Where would you like to grow and how can you do so?

2. Adapted from plural to singular.

a prayer when considering death

Casting Anchors: Poet Unknown

Ever since sin entered this world, death has been a universal experience. None of us can escape it, none of us can avoid it. We must all come to the end of our lives, die, and face divine judgment. Though we may seek to deny the inevitability of death and do all we can to hold it off, our time will most certainly come. And for that reason we must consider death. We must contemplate the fact that we will die and must contemplate the state in which we wish to die. We must contemplate the wonderful reality that God does not leave us ignorant but tells us how death can be a great deliverance—a deliverance from sin, sadness, sickness, and all that grieves us in this world. With God's strong hand holding us, we can pass safely through death to endless delights in his presence.

observe

The author capitalizes a number of different words throughout the poem: Patience, Faith, Hope, Love. Each of these is one of the "anchors" he relies upon to secure him in the storm—to give him confidence in the Lord as he considers the reality of death.

pray

The night is dark, but God, my God,
Is here and in command;
And sure am I, when morning breaks,
I shall be "at the land."
And since I know the darkness is
To him as sunniest day,
I cast my anchor Patience out,
And wish, but wait for day.

Fierce drives the storm, but winds and waves
Within His hand are held,
And trusting in Omnipotence,
My fears are sweetly quelled.
If wrecked, I'm in His faithful grasp,
I'll trust Him though He slay;

So letting go the anchor Faith,
I'll wish, but wait for day.

Still seem the moments dreary, long?
I rest upon the Lord;
I muse on His "eternal years,"
And feast upon His word.
His promises, so rich, so great,
Are my support and stay;
I'll drop the anchor Hope ahead,
And wish, but wait for day.

O wisdom infinite! O light
And love supreme, Divine!
How can I feel one fluttering doubt,
In hands so dear as Thine!
I'll lean on Thee, my best Beloved,
My heart on Thy heart lay
And casting out the anchor Love,
I'll wish, but wait for day.

—Poet Unknown, "Casting Anchors"

reflect

Philippians 1:21–26; Hebrews 9:27–28.

apply

Even for the Christian, the prospect of death can be intimidating or even terrifying. Are you afraid to die? What can you do to increase your confidence as you face death's inevitability?

a prayer of praise for God's works and ways

Praise: Horatius Bonar

It is good to give thanks to the LORD, to sing praises to your name, O Most High" (Ps. 92:1). Here the psalmist tells God what is so demonstrably true—that it is a joy and a pleasure to give thanks to him and to praise his name. God created us for the purpose of worshiping him and it is good and fitting that we do so. For when we praise God, we are giving him his due, giving him the recognition he deserves. What should we praise God for? For creating this world and sustaining it, for sending his Son and sending his Spirit, for saving people and sanctifying them, and for so much else besides. Truly, we will never run out of reasons to praise God and worship his most holy name. We can praise him from now to the deepest depths of eternity and we will never run out of reasons to express our amazement at who he is and what he has done.

observe

Horatius Bonar was a Scottish pastor and hymn-writer who lived from 1808 to 1889 (and who is not to be confused with his brother Andrew, who was a prominent Christian leader in his own right). Over the course of a long ministry, Horatius wrote many hymns and poems, the best known of which are "I Heard the Voice of Jesus Say" and "I Was a Wandering Sheep." His works remain popular and accessible to this day.

pray

Praises to Him who built the hills;
Praises to Him the streams who fills;
Praises to Him who lights each star
That sparkles in the blue afar.

Praises to Him who makes the morn,
And bids it glow with beams new-born;
Who draws the shadows of the night,
Like curtains, o'er my wearied sight.

Praises to Him whose love has given,
In Christ His Son, the Life of heaven;
Who for my darkness gives me light,
And turns to day my deepest night.

Praises to Him, in grace who came,
To bear my woe, and sin, and shame;
Who lived to die, who died to rise,
The God-accepted sacrifice.

Praises to Him the chain who broke,
Opened the prison, burst the yoke,
Sent forth its captives, glad and free,
Heirs of an endless liberty.

Praises to Him who sheds abroad
Within my heart the love of God;
The Spirit of all truth and peace,
Fountain of joy and holiness!

The Father, Son, and Spirit, now
The hands I lift, the knees I bow;
To Jah-Jehovah thus I raise
The sinner's song of endless praise.

—Horatius Bonar, "Praise"[1]

reflect

Psalm 92:1–4; Psalm 147.

---

1. Adapted from plural to singular.

apply

When you pray, do you find yourself more naturally praising God or petitioning God—expressing your wonder at who he is and what he has done, or expressing your needs and desires? What might this say about the posture of your heart before the Lord?

a prayer of trust in God's sovereignty

God's Decrees: John Ryland

God reveals himself in Scripture as sovereign. *Sovereign* is a word of supremacy and authority. God is supreme over this world—he is superior to every other being—because he is the one who existed before the world and who created the world. God also has full authority over this world and over every person and every creature who lives within it. This means he has the right to give orders and to hold us accountable to them. It also means that he has the right to determine events and actions and to ensure they take place as he has prescribed. If this is true, then we can always be confident that it is ultimately God our loving Father who determines the circumstances of our lives, whether we are sick or healthy, rich or poor, whether we are enjoying times of great pleasure or enduring times of great grief. No matter what, he is the Sovereign Ruler.

observe

In the final stanza the poet uses the word "bereavèd." An accented *è* like this is meant to indicate that the closing "ed" should be pronounced like the name Ed. This adds a syllable to the word, thus preserving the poem's meter. Hence, you should read "be-REEV-ed" rather than "be-REEVD."

pray

Sovereign Ruler of the skies,
Ever gracious, ever wise;
All my times are in Thy hand,
All events at Thy command.

His decree who formed the earth
Fixed my first and second birth;
Parents, native place, and time,
All appointed were by Him.

He that formed me in the womb,
He shall guide me to the tomb:

All my times shall ever be
Ordered by His wise decree.

Times of sickness; times of health;
Times of penury[1] and wealth;
Times of trial and of grief;
Times of triumph and relief;

Times the tempter's power to prove;
Times to taste the Saviour's love;
All must come, and last, and end,
As shall please my heavenly Friend.

Plagues and deaths around me fly;
Till He bids, I cannot die;
Not a single shaft can hit,
Till the God of love sees fit.

O Thou Gracious, Wise and Just,
In Thy hands my life I trust:
Have I somewhat[2] dearer still?
I resign it to Thy will.

May I always own Thy hand
Still to the surrender stand;

1. Extreme poverty.
2. Something.

Know that Thou art God alone,
I and mine are all Thine own.

Thee, at all times, will I bless;
Having Thee, I all possess;
How can I bereavèd be,
Since I cannot part with Thee?

—John Ryland, "God's Decrees"

reflect

Isaiah 40:9–17; Isaiah 46:8–11.

apply

When you consider God's sovereignty, do you find yourself comforted? Intimidated? Angry? Why is it so important to consider God's sovereignty alongside his other attributes such as his wisdom, his holiness, and his goodness?

a prayer for times of affliction

Discipline:
George Herbert

One of the difficult truths Christians face is that there are times when our sin and disobedience leads God to chastise us, to bring upon us some form of discipline meant to steer us away from our sin and back into obedience to him. God treats us this way not out of anger or spite but out of love. He is treating us as beloved children, for as the author to the letter to the Hebrews asks, "What son is there whom his father does not discipline?" A short time later he explains God's purpose in it: "For the moment all discipline seems painful rather than pleasant, but later it yields the peaceful fruit of righteousness to those who have been trained by it"

(Heb. 12:7, 11). There may be many reasons we undergo a trial or a time of suffering, but in humility we should be willing to prayerfully ask God if he may be alerting us to sin we refuse to confess or put to death.

observe

This prayer assumes you have become convinced that the suffering you are experiencing—suffering of body, mind, or soul—is related to a sin you have now identified and confessed. It pleads with God to remove his hand of discipline for the sake of love.

pray

Throw away Thy rod,
Throw away Thy wrath:
O my God,
Take the gentle path.

For my heart's desire
Unto Thine is bent:
I aspire
To a full consent.

Not a word or look
I affect to own,
But by book,
And Thy book alone.

Though I fail, I weep:
Though I halt in pace,
Yet I creep
To the throne of grace.

Then let wrath remove;
Love will do the deed:
For with love
Stony hearts will bleed.

Love is swift of foot;
Love's a man of war,
And can shoot,
And can hit from far.

Who can 'scape[1] His bow?
That which wrought on Thee,
Brought Thee low,
Needs must[2] work on me.

---

1. Escape.
2. "Needs must" is an antiquated phrase that means "necessarily must."

Throw away Thy rod;
Though man frailties hath,
Thou art God:
Throw away Thy wrath.

—George Herbert, "Discipline"

reflect

Proverbs 13:24; Hebrews 12:1–11.

apply

It is important to distinguish between punishment for sin (which was fully satisfied by Christ in his death on the cross) and chastisement (which is a consequence for sin that God may bring into our lives for our own good). Does it bother you that God may chastise you due to unidentified or unconfessed sin? What are some ways you might be able to analyze a time of suffering to determine whether it may be the consequence of sin or some other cause entirely?

a prayer to desire and delight in God

Devout Aspirations: John Quarles

When God saves us by his grace, he begins a remarkable work of reformation within us. We quickly learn that he is changing us from the inside out. We might be tempted to think he would be content with outward transformation—with cleaner words, better behavior, and diminished addictions. But he means to accomplish something so much more real, so much more thorough, so much more authentic. He means to transform us at the level of the heart, the level of our deepest longings and closest desires. Soon we find that what had previously been desirable has become undesirable and what was previously unthinkable is now the very thing we long and pray for. We find that God gives us holy and devout aspirations—aspirations to fear him, love him, serve him, obey him, and do all things for his glory.

observe

This is a slightly longer and more complicated poem than many in this collection. But read it carefully and repeatedly and see how the poet pleads with God for better and purer spiritual aspirations.

pray

Great God, whose sceptre rules the earth,
Distil Thy fear into my heart;
That being rapt[1] with holy mirth
I may proclaim how good Thou art:
Open my lips, that I may sing
Full praises to my God, my King.

Great God, Thy garden is defac'd,
The weeds thrive there, Thy flowers decay;
O call to mind Thy promise past,
Restore Thou these, cut those away:

1. Enraptured or elated.

Till then let not the weeds have power
To starve or stunt the poorest flower.

In all extremes, Lord, Thou art still
The Mount whereto my hopes do flee;
O make my soul detest all ill,
Because so much abhorr'd by Thee:
Lord, let Thy gracious trials show
That I am just, or make me so.

Fountain of light and living breath,
Whose mercies never fail nor fade,
Fill me with life that hath no death;
Fill me with light that hath no shade;
Appoint the remnant of my days
To see Thy power and sing Thy praise.

Lord God of gods, before whose throne
Stand storms and fire! O what shall we
Return to Heaven, that is our own,
When all the world belongs to Thee?
We have no offering to impart,
But praises, and a wounded heart.

O Thou that sitt'st in Heaven, and seest
My deeds without, my thoughts within,
Be Thou my prince, be Thou my priest—

Command my soul, and cure my sin:
How bitter my afflictions be
I care not, so I rise to Thee.

What I possess, or what I crave,
Brings no content, great God, to me.
If what I would, or what I have,
Be not possest, and blest in Thee:
What I enjoy, O make it mine,
In making me—that have it—Thine.

When winter-fortunes cloud the brows
Of summer-friends,—when eyes grow strange,—
When plighted[2] faith forgets its vows,
When earth and all things in it change,—
O Lord, Thy mercies fail me never,—
Where Thou lovest, Thou lovest for ever.

Great God, whose kingdom hath no end,
Into whose secrets none can dive,
Whose mercy none can apprehend,
Whose justice none can feel—and live,
What my dull heart cannot aspire
To know, Lord, teach me to admire.

—John Quarles, "Devout Aspirations"

2. Promised.

reflect

2 Corinthians 5:17; Romans 12:2.

apply

In what ways have you seen your desires and aspirations transformed since you became a Christian? What sinful desires and aspirations remain that you continue to bring before the Lord to seek his forgiveness and transformation? If you sense your desire for God growing cold, what images or sections of this poem can you call to mind to stir your zeal for God again?

a prayer for pondering the cross of Christ

Good Friday: Christina Rossetti

It is good for us to take time to pause to consider the cross of Christ—to consider the wonder of the Son of God taking upon himself the sin of man and suffering its penalty. It is good for us to consider that "for our sake he made him to be sin who knew no sin, so that in him we might become the righteousness of God" (2 Cor. 5:21). It is good for us to consider the love that would be willing to endure such distress and such agony so we could be saved. And having done that, it is good for us to confess how often this historical and spiritual reality fails to thrill us, fails to keep us from the sin that made it necessary, fails to motivate us to live for the glory of God, and fails to move our hardened hearts to express themselves in tears of sorrow, wonder, and worship. This prayer ends with a request that Jesus, the true Shepherd, would break the hardness of our hearts to truly grieve our sin, paid for by Christ.

observe

Be sure to look for and find the unusual rhyme scheme. And be equally sure to look for and find the list of people, beings, and objects who were moved in worshipful wonder by the sight of Christ's suffering for you and me.

pray

Am I a stone, and not a sheep,
That I can stand, O Christ, beneath Thy cross,
To number drop by drop Thy blood's slow loss,
And yet not weep?
Not so those women loved
Who with exceeding grief lamented Thee;
Not so fallen Peter, weeping bitterly;
Not so the thief was moved;
Not so the Sun and Moon
Which hid their faces in a starless sky,
A horror of great darkness at broad noon—
I, only I.
Yet give not o'er,

But seek Thy sheep, true Shepherd of the flock;
Greater than Moses, turn and look once more
And smite a rock.

—Christina Rossetti, "Good Friday"

reflect

Romans 8:32; Galatians 3:13.

apply

How often do you find yourself feeling apathetic about Christ's work on the cross compared to how often you find your soul thrilled by it? What are some practices you have found helpful to keep your soul fixated on Christ's suffering, death, and substitutionary sacrifice?

a prayer for pondering weakness and mortality

My Times Are in Thy Hands: Christopher Newman Hall

We are weak and finite beings. Created from the dust, we live, die, and then return to the dust. As the Preacher said long ago, "The dust returns to the earth as it was, and the spirit returns to God who gave it." Little wonder, then, that "vanity of vanities, says the Preacher; all is vanity" (Eccl. 12:7–8). This world has many joys to offer us, and God means for us to appreciate and enjoy them. But we must never forget that they are temporary and fleeting, because eventually God will call us out of this world and into judgment. Between the moment of our birth and the moment of our death, our times are in God's hands. We have no knowledge of the future and, despite our best efforts, no ability to control it. It is far better, then, to entrust it to the God who knows "the end from the beginning and from ancient times things not yet done," the one who proclaims, "My counsel shall stand, and I will accomplish all my purpose" (Isa. 46:10).

observe

Observe how each stanza begins with the same line—every stanza, that is, until the final one. Consider why the poet makes the change at the end.

pray

My times are in Thy hand!
I know not what a day
Or e'en an hour may bring to me,
But I am safe while trusting Thee,
Though all things fade away.
All weakness, I
On Him rely
Who fixed the earth and spread the starry sky.

My times are in Thy hand!
Pale poverty or wealth.
Corroding care or calm repose.

Spring's balmy breath or winter's snows.
Sickness or buoyant health,—
Whate'er betide,
If God provide,
'Tis for the best; I wish no lot beside.

My times are in Thy hand!
Should friendship pure illume
And strew my path with fairest flowers,
Or should I spend life's dreary hours
In solitude's dark gloom,
Thou art a friend.
Till time shall end
Unchangeably the same; in Thee all
beauties blend.

My times are in Thy hand!
Many or few, my days
I leave with Thee,—this only pray,
That by Thy grace, I, every day
Devoting to Thy praise,
May ready be
To welcome Thee
Whene'er Thou com'st to set my spirit free.

My times are in Thy hand!
Howe'er those times may end,

Sudden or slow my soul's release,
Midst anguish, frenzy, or in peace,
I'm safe with Christ my friend.
If He is nigh,
Howe'er I die,
'Twill be the dawn of heavenly ecstasy.

My times are in Thy hand!
To Thee I can entrust
My slumbering clay, till Thy command
Bids all the dead before Thee stand,
Awaking from the dust.
Beholding Thee,
What bliss 't will be
With all Thy saints to spend eternity!

To spend eternity
In heaven's unclouded light!
From sorrow, sin, and frailty free,
Beholding and resembling Thee,—
O too transporting sight!
Prospect too fair
For flesh to bear!
Haste! haste! my Lord, and soon transport
me there!

—Christopher Newman Hall, "My Times Are in Thy Hands"

reflect

Psalm 31:14–18; Proverbs 19:21.

apply

How do you trust God with your future? Do you praise him, as this prayer reminds us, that your times are in his hands? How might this change your understanding of future suffering, sorrow, or trials?

a prayer asking God to illumine his word

Father of Mercies, in Thy Word: Anne Steele

Though we have been saved by God and indwelled by the Holy Spirit, we remain dependent upon God to teach us how to please and honor him. Though we read the Bible eagerly and hungrily, still we know that for us to derive any benefit from it we must have his help. Thus, as we open the Bible in our times of personal or family devotion, or when the preacher opens it to proclaim its truths, we should always prepare ourselves to hear it by asking God to illumine it to us—to open our minds to understand it, to open our hearts to receive it, and to open our hands to obey whatever God commands us. Perhaps best of all we should echo the psalmist and pray that his words would be true of us: "Oh how I love your law! It is my meditation all the day" (Ps. 119:97). For if we truly love God's Word, we will most surely obey God's Word.

observe

Anne Steele (1717–1778) was a Baptist hymn-writer who wrote her earliest works under the pseudonym Theodosia. Because she never married or had children, she devoted much of her life to writing and contemplation. The personal relationship she fostered with the Lord is evident in her hymns. Though relatively few of those hymns continue to be sung today, she was during her life among the most accomplished female hymn-writers.

pray

Father of mercies, in Thy word
What endless glory shines!
Forever be Thy name adored
For these celestial lines.

Here may the blind and hungry come,
And light and food receive;
Here shall the lowliest guest have room,
And taste and see and live.

Here springs of consolation rise
To cheer the fainting mind,
And thirsting souls receive supplies,
And sweet refreshment find.

Here the Redeemer's welcome voice
Spreads heavenly peace around,
And life and everlasting joys
Attend the blissful sound.

O may these hallowed pages be
My ever dear delight,
And still new beauties may I see,
And still increasing light.

Divine instructor, gracious Lord,
Be Thou forever near;
Teach me to love Thy sacred word,
And view my Savior here.

—Anne Steele, "Father of
Mercies, in Thy Word"

reflect

Psalm 119:33–40; 2 Timothy 3:16–17.

apply

Why do we need the illumination of God's Spirit to love and understand his Word to us? Do you love the Bible? Can you echo the psalmist as he expresses his soul's longing to commune with God through the Bible? If not, what practices could you integrate into your life that might help?

a prayer for hard times

Hard Times: George MacDonald

There are times in life when our souls are weary and downcast, times when we are sad and may not even know why. Our natural desire is to pass quickly through such a time of sorrow and emerge as soon as possible into joys beyond. Yet it may do us good to pause to ask ourselves this: "Why are you cast down, O my soul, and why are you in turmoil within me?" (Ps. 42:5). Not all sadness is wrong, and not all sadness is meant to be immediately overcome. We may be sad because we are burdened with cares that we ought to unburden on the Lord; we may be sad because we have sinned and have failed to confess it; we may be sad simply because we are weak and life is difficult. Even in our sadness it does us good to wait upon the Lord and to meditate on his Word even as we preach to our souls, "Hope in God; for I shall again praise him, my salvation" (Ps. 42:5).

observe

This poem begins with the author describing his condition to the Lord before he begins to submit that sorrow to his care. He does not wish to rush through the time of sorrow lest he miss some good God may mean to do in him through it. He will not force happiness by pursuing worldly pleasures but will wait until God sparks divine happiness.

pray

I am weary, and very lonely,
And can but think—think.
If there were some water only
That a spirit might drink—drink,

And arise,
With light in the eyes
And a crown of hope on the brow,
To walk abroad in the strength of gladness,
Not sit in the house, benumbed with sadness—
As now!

But, Lord, Thy child will be sad—
As sad as it pleases Thee;
Will sit, not seeking to be glad,

Till Thou bid sadness flee,
And, drawing near,
With Thy good cheer
Awake Thy life in me.

—George MacDonald, "Hard Times"

reflect

Psalm 42; Psalm 63.

apply

Can you remember a time when God was accomplishing something through your sorrow? What might you have missed if you had rushed through your sorrow without deliberately taking it to the Lord?

a prayer for the salvation of the lost

We Pray for Those Who Do Not Pray: Christopher Newman Hall

Having come to Christ by faith, we find ourselves longing to see our loved ones come to him as well. We long for them to see the perilous state of their souls, to see the beauty of Jesus Christ, and to believe in the gospel. No sooner do we learn to pray than we begin to make this request known to God. We pray that he would convict them of their sin, that he would give them a godly sorrow for their rebellion against him, and that he would lead them to cry out for mercy. We pray that God would soften their hearts of stone and give them hearts of flesh so they can receive the good news of what Christ has done. We do this with a humble confidence, convinced that God alone can bring a person to the point of repentance, but convinced also that it is his great joy to save the lost, for God does not wish "that any should perish, but that all should reach repentance" (2 Peter 3:9).

observe

Christopher Newman Hall, known also simply as Newman Hall, was an English Nonconformist minister who pastored in the mid- to late-1800s. He was known as an especially talented preacher. A committed abolitionist, he labored for the end of slavery in the United States, often traveling to America to make his case. He wrote a number of books, one of which, *Pilgrim Songs*, is a collection of what he termed "rhythmical meditations."

pray

I pray for those who do not pray!
Who waste away salvation's day;
For those I love who love not Thee—
My grief, their danger, pitying see.

Those for whom many tears are shed
And blessings breathed upon their head,

The children of Thy people save
From godless life and hopeless grave.

Hear fathers, mothers, as they pray
For sons, for daughters, far away—
Brother for brother, friend for friend—
Hear all our prayers that upward blend.

I pray for those who long have heard
But still neglect Thy gracious Word;
Soften the hearts obdurate[1] made
By calls unheeded; vows delayed.

Release the drunkard from his chain,
Bare those beguiled by pleasure vain,
Set free the slaves of lust, and bring
Back to their home the wandering.

The hopeless cheer; guide those who doubt;
Restore the lost; cast no one out;
For all that are far off I pray,
Since I was once far off as they.

—Christopher Newman Hall, "We Pray for Those Who Do Not Pray"[2]

1. Stubborn and obstinate.
2. Adapted from plural to singular.

reflect

2 Peter 3:8–10; Luke 15:3–7.

apply

Do you pray for your loved ones who do not yet know the Lord? And do you pray with a humble confidence, trusting that it is God's great delight to seek and save the lost? Is there any sense in which you think you were somehow more deserving to receive God's mercy or more likely to be a recipient of it? As you pray this prayer, have one or two specific individuals in mind.

a prayer for God's guidance

Savior, Lead Me: Charles Ebert Orr

Life brings us to many crossroads, to many situations in which we must decide whether to turn to the left or to the right, to follow this path or that. As we face such choices, God is good to give us guidance through his Word and his Spirit, to influence us toward decisions that honor him. Our tendency in such times is to choose the path that looks easiest—that looks like it will provide the fewest challenges and the greatest joys. Yet our foremost concern should never be for our own ease; rather, it should be for God to be glorified in and through us. We should be willing to go anywhere and do anything for the sake of the Lord, knowing that he will be with us, guiding, directing, and blessing us. Hence, the Christian's prayer ought to be "God, I will do whatever glorifies your name, provided Christ promises to remain present with me."

observe

Orr uses the phrase "flow'ry beds of ease." He draws this from Isaac Watts's famous work "Am I a Soldier of the Cross," in which he asks, "Must I be carried to the skies / on flow'ry beds of ease, / while others fought to win the prize, / and sailed thro' bloody seas?" Orr uses some of the same lines and metaphors, so he clearly means for his poem to complement Watts's.

pray

I do not pray that life be spent
On flow'ry beds of ease;
I only pray that Christ may guide
Across the stormy seas.

I do not pray that flow'rs may bloom
Along my pilgrim way;
I only ask that Christ may guide
My footsteps lest I stray.

If Thou wilt lead me by the hand,
And guide my trembling feet,
For Thee, O Christ, I'll gladly drink
The bitter with the sweet.

What though my life be peace or pain,
'Twill only soon be o'er;
I want to walk the way that leads
To heav'n's eternal shore.

—Charles Ebert Orr, "Savior, Lead Me"

reflect

Psalm 23; Isaiah 43:2.

apply

Is it your deepest desire to honor God, even if it requires difficulty, pain, or suffering? Or does your desire to serve God end right at the point at which he may call you to endure suffering? Can you say, with the poet, "For Thee, O Christ, I'll gladly drink the bitter with the sweet"? Reflect today on the joy and necessity of following Christ wherever he may lead you.

a prayer that we would forgive as we have been forgiven

The Test: Mary B. Sleight

The Lord asks many difficult things of those who are his. He asks them to forsake their sins and to pursue holiness; he asks them to be willing to turn away from even their own family if that is what it takes to follow him; he asks them to steward their money toward his purposes instead of spending it on their own desires. But perhaps the most difficult thing of all is to forgive—to forgive those who have hurt us, harmed us, and done us wrong. In the Lord's Prayer we ask God to "forgive us our sins, for we ourselves forgive everyone who is indebted to us" (Luke 11:4). As people who have been freely and graciously forgiven by God, we must now extend forgiveness to others—to extend to them the very same mercy that God has seen fit to extend to us. This is no small challenge, yet one we must joyfully undertake for the sake of our commitment to the one who has forgiven us.

observe

Many great poems display a kind of narrative flow in which they introduce a concern or problem and then work toward a resolution. Look for the poet's concern in the first two stanzas and observe how she works toward a satisfying resolution by the closing lines.

pray

"Forgive our debts as we forgive,"
Ah, who, dear Lord, can pray that prayer?
The rest with ready zeal is said,
But self-accused I falter there,
Conscious, beneath its crucial test,
Of hate my lips have ne'er confessed.

As we forgive! O Christ in Heaven
Can I both pardon and forget,
When arrows dipped in deadly gall
Within my heart are rankling yet?—

Sharp arrows by the false hands aimed
Of those who once love's largess claimed.

Be pitiful, O blessed Christ,
Nor chide me for my bitter thought
Of those who rendered hate for love,
And mocked me for the gifts I brought,
For Thou, alone, dear Lord, dost know
Flow measureless the debt I owe.

Forgive us, Lord. Can theirs exceed
The endless debt I owe to Thee?
Thy patient, unrequited love,
Thy mercy, boundless as the sea,
Thy life blood, poured in healing balm
From wounded side and nail-pierced palm.

Ashamed and penitent I kneel;
O Thou, who dost my sins forget,
Help me with Thy sweet charity
To pardon freely all the debt,
That praying, Lord, that prayer again,
My grateful heart may say "Amen."

—Mary B. Sleight, "The Test"[1]

1. Adapted from plural to singular.

reflect

Luke 7:41–50; Luke 11:1–4.

apply

Have you ever struggled to forgive someone? Why was it so difficult? Is there anyone you are currently refusing to forgive? If so, join in this prayer and ask God to help you forgive others with the same joy and completeness with which God has forgiven you. Reflect on how our ability to forgive is only possible because God has first forgiven us such a great debt we owe.

a prayer to the Holy Spirit

Hymn to the Holy Spirit: Poet Unknown

As Christians we proclaim that God is triune. Though there is one God, this God is three persons, each of them equal in power, authority, majesty, and every other divine attribute. What distinguishes these three persons are their roles. Though we most often pray to the Father (as Jesus taught us), there are times when it is good to pray to the Son or the Spirit—to pray that they would bless us in accordance with their roles within the Godhead. As it pertains to salvation, God the Father is the one who planned our salvation, Jesus is the one who achieved it through his death and resurrection, and the Holy Spirit is the one who applies it through sanctification. So we may pray to the Holy Spirit to ask him to make our hearts receptive to God's Word, to put sin to death, to kindle within us good and noble desires, to help us love God more, and to rest ever more in the powerful gospel.

observe

Read carefully to see the poet's progression from the calming of the mind to a rekindling of the flame of desire for God. Then consider how this progression powerfully models how we ought to pray.

pray

Come, Holy Spirit, calm my mind,
And fit me to approach my God;
Remove each vain, each worldly thought,
And lead me to Thy blest abode.

Hast Thou imparted to my soul
A living spark of holy fire?
Oh! kindle now the sacred flame,
Make me to burn with pure desire.

Impress upon my wandering heart
The love that Christ to sinners bore;

Then, mourn the wounds my sins produced,
And my redeeming God adore.

A brighter faith and hope impart,
And let me now my Saviour see;
Oh! soothe and cheer my burdened heart,
And bid my spirit rest in Thee.

—Poet Unknown, "Hymn to the Holy Spirit"

reflect

John 16:4–15; John 16:23–24.

apply

Why might we choose to pray to one person of the Trinity instead of another? In what situations might it be appropriate to pray to the Son or to the Spirit? Why do you think the author of this poem chose to address the Holy Spirit?

a prayer of repentance

What Am I, Lord? Emily Spear

At times every Christian is overwhelmed by the reality of what God has done for us in Christ—overwhelmed that God called us out of darkness and into light and overwhelmed that we have been given the gift of faith. Who are we to be the objects of such mercy? Who are we to be called sons and daughters of God? Who are we to be able to look forward to such sure and wonderful promises? How should we respond? We should respond with worship and with obedience. We should respond by worshiping God for his goodness and for the wonder of being known and saved by him. And we should respond by joyfully obeying him—by putting sin to death and coming alive to righteousness, by consecrating our lives to his service. And all of this not to earn our salvation or to repay it, but simply because he is so very worthy.

observe

Notice that the poet begins the first two stanzas by contrasting her status apart from Christ to her status as one who has been clothed and loved by Christ. This contrast continues, leading her to a deeper love and appreciation of the grace and mercy that God has shown to her.

pray

Oh! what am I, so slight a thing,
To wear the image of my King?
Oh! what am I, that I be saved
And in Thy crimson fountain laved,[1]
The blessed promise to receive,
And by the grace of God believe?

Oh! what am I that I am loved
By Jesus Christ? That I am moved
A full confession now to make
And give my life for Jesus' sake?
My life I cannot give. Ah! no;
For all my life to Thee I owe.

---

1. Washed.

Unclean and vile, my heart doth moan,
And saddens o'er Thy dying groan;
Yet I can still relinquish sin,
And at the portals enter in,
Though of myself I cannot bring
To deck Thy crown the slightest thing.

A life of lowliness and love,
For Thy dear sake, shall soar above:
It is the least that I can do,
My fleeting years, though short and few,
I can, and will lay at Thy feet,
And serve Thee while my pulses beat.

—Emily Spear, "What Am I, Lord?"[2]

reflect

Galatians 4:4–7; Colossians 3:5.

apply

What value might there be in contrasting who we are apart from Christ with who we now are as his beloved? How might

2. Adapted slightly.

this kind of reflection grow and deepen your love for God? When was the last time you found yourself overwhelmed by the reality that God saved you from your sins? What might it say about you if this is a rare experience, and how might this poem aid you in growing in the wonder of what Christ has accomplished for you?

a prayer of confident submission to God

Thy Way Is Best: Christopher Newman Hall

The first sin of the first human beings was one of rebellion when they determined they would do what they desired instead of submitting to what God had commanded. Since then, each one of us has felt the same desire and faced the same temptation. We believe we know better than God and that life would be better if it was done our way instead of his. "My way, not Thine" is the cry of our sinful hearts. But as we grow in our faith and as the Spirit carries out his work of sanctification, we learn that God has higher purposes in this world than our comfort and better things to accomplish than we could ever ask or even imagine. As we come to trust God more and as we long to see him honored and glorified, we find a new prayer in our hearts: "Thy way, not mine." For we know that there is no desire purer than his, no will better than his, and no way that will bring him greater glory. Even in times of sorrow and loss, times of pain and uncertainty our prayer becomes "Thy way, O Lord! Thy way—not mine!"

observe

The poet begins with confident proclamations that God's way is best. Yet then a time of pain comes upon him and he begins to wonder whether that can truly be the case: "Can Thy way be best?" By the end, however, his confidence is restored, and though he cannot fully see or understand, he once again proclaims, "Thy way is best."

pray

Thy way, O Lord! Thy way—not mine!
Although, opprest,
For smoother, sunnier paths I pine,
Thy way is best.

Though crossing thirsty deserts drear,
Or mountain's crest;
Although I faint with toil and fear,
Thy way is best.

Though not one open door befriend
The passing guest;
Though night its darkest terror lend,
Thy way is best.

So seeming wild without a plan,
Now east, now west,
Joys born and slain, hopes blighted, can
Thy way be best?

My soul by grief seems not to be
More pure and blest;
Alas! I cannot, cannot see
Thy way is best.

I cannot see—on every hand
By anguish prest,
In vain I try to understand
Thy way is best.

But I believe—Thy life and death,
Thy love attest,

And every promise clearly saith[1]—
"Thy way is best."

I cannot see—but I believe;
If heavenly rest
Is reached by roads where most I grieve,
Thy way is best.

—Christopher Newman Hall, "Thy Way Is Best"

reflect

Matthew 26:39; Philippians 1:12–14.

apply

Have you ever had a time when you believed God's way was best but just could not see or understand how your present circumstances were that best? What are some of the situations in your life when you believed your way was better than God's? How did God eventually convince you that his way was best? What has he taught you since then?

1. Says (pronounced "seth").

a prayer for deliverance from temptation

Without and Within:
M. A. B. Kelly

To live in this world is to be tempted. There is no path through life that does not involve facing the temptation to commit sins. Even Jesus Christ was tempted: he was tempted by Satan to forsake the will of the Father and to take an easier path through life—"Just bow before me and I will give you all the kingdoms of this world," the devil told him. Satan promised the reward of the cross without the pain of the cross. Yet Jesus remained confident in the Father's plan that the kingdom would come not apart from pain but through it and because of it. Jesus responded to temptation with "Be gone, Satan!" Jesus endured the temptation to forsake the will of God and through his obedience has given us the power to endure similar temptation. "Because he himself has suffered when tempted, he is able to help those who are being tempted" (Heb. 2:18).

observe

Notice how the poet uses the imagery of sunlight as a metaphor for freedom from sin. The sustained contrast between the darkness of sin and the longing for sunlight to drive away the darkness calls to mind the drawing back of thick curtains that have covered a window and kept the light from flooding in.

pray

The sun shines in my outer world,
But darkness reigns within,
A fearful gloom enshrouds my soul,
The nebula of sin.
Dear Savior, smile away this gloom,
And let the sunlight in.

Sweet bird-songs cheer my outer world,
But anguish wails within.

Ambition, pride, and gross deceit
Have bound my soul in sin;
Then, O my Savior, break these bonds,
And let the sunlight in!

Temptations throng my way without,
Remorse broods dark within;
The chains that bind my tortured soul
Are festered o'er with sin;
Dear Savior, send Thy healing balm,
And let the sunlight in.

While pleasure gayly smiles without,
What torment reigns within!
And still, poor weakling that I am,
I tread the paths of sin,
My Savior, I am lost if Thou
Let not the sunlight in.

—M. A. B. Kelly, "Without and Within"

reflect

Hebrews 2:18; 1 Corinthians 10:13.

apply

Each stanza ends with a different request to our Savior: the smile of a loving friend, the breaking of bonds holding us prisoner, a healing balm from festering sickness, and a guide to rescue us from our lost wanderings. Which of these images speaks to your battle with sin most clearly today? Why do you think we fail to take hold of God's power in our battle against sin, a power that is available in the very moment we are tempted?

a prayer for Christ's return

Jesus, Return: Henry Van Dyke

The gospel is a holistic message that encompasses the past, present, and future. We *have been saved* when we put our faith in Christ; we *are being saved* as the Holy Spirit renews us from within; and we *will be saved* when Christ returns. His return will mark the utmost sorrow for those who have rejected him, for they will be sent away to everlasting judgment. But his return will mark the utmost joy for those who have accepted him, for they will be drawn to everlasting life. And while there are many wonderful benefits that will be ours—the end of all pain and sorrow, the coming of full and final justice, the eradication of even the smallest desire to sin—the greatest blessing of all is that we will be with Christ. The Savior we now see by faith we will see by sight and together we will worship and praise his name. No wonder, then, that the cry of Christians of every age has been "Maranatha! Christ, come quickly!"

observe

Observe the different images the poet uses in this poem—flowers that need light after darkness, lamps that light a lonely road, a heavy yoke that must be carried a long way.

pray

Return, dear Lord, to those who look
With eager eyes that yearn
For Thee among the garden flowers;
After the dark and lonely hours,
As morning light return.

Return to those who wander far,
With lamps that dimly burn,
Along the troubled road of thought,
Where doubt and conflict come unsought,—
With inward joy return.

Return to those on whom the yoke
Of life is hard and stern;

Renew the hope within their breast,
Draw them to Thee and give them rest;
O Friend of Man, return.

Return to this war-weary world,
And help us all to learn
Thy secret of victorious life,
The love that triumphs over strife,—
O prince of Peace, return.

Jesus, I ask not now that day
When all men shall discern
Thy coming with the angelic host;
Today, to all who need Thee most,
In silent ways, return!

—Henry Van Dyke,
"Jesus, Return"[1]

reflect

1 Corinthians 15:20–27; Philippians 3:12–16.

---

1. Adapted from plural to singular.

apply

Do you long for the return of Jesus Christ? Do you consistently pray for it? Can you honestly say that as you consider the return of Christ you most anticipate Christ himself or merely the benefits that Christ brings? In the final stanza, the poet prays not for the future return of Christ but for Christ to return "in silent ways" to those in need today. Where in your life do you most need Christ to return and bring his presence afresh?

a prayer to pray when distracted

Ah! Dearest Lord, I Cannot Pray: F. W. Faber

We live in an age of distraction, an age in which the world around us seems set on drawing our attention away from what we wish to do and toward a hundred things that are more urgent, more appealing, or more entertaining. Yet as we read the works of our forebears, we learn that distraction is a condition that transcends time and place, for Christians have always struggled to pray without having their minds and hearts diverted toward matters of lesser importance. Rather than pretending the situation is otherwise and that we are better than we are, perhaps we should begin our times of devotion by asking God to give us minds that are focused and hearts that desire to commune with him in prayer. As a distressed father once said to Jesus, "I believe; help my unbelief!" (Mark 9:24), perhaps we should cry, "I believe in prayer, so help me pray!"

observe

The poet begins by acknowledging that his mind is distracted and his body restless as he tries to pray—realities that are all too familiar to each of us. He confesses this but does not quit. Instead he continues in prayer knowing that the Lord meets weak sinners as they seek him in their struggle against sin.

pray

Ah! dearest Lord, I cannot pray,
My fancy is not free;
Unmannerly distractions come,
And force my thoughts from Thee.

My very flesh has restless fits;
My changeful limbs conspire
With all these phantoms of the mind
My inner self to tire.

I cannot pray; yet, Lord! Thou knowst
The pain it is to me
To have my vainly struggling thoughts
Thus torn away from Thee.

Yet Thou art oft present, Lord!
In weak distracted prayer:
A sinner out of heart with self
Most often finds Thee there.

My Saviour! why should I complain
And why fear aught but sin?
Distractions are but outward things;
Thy peace dwells far within.

—F. W. Faber, "Ah! Dearest Lord, I Cannot Pray"[1]

reflect

Luke 5:16; Luke 11:1–4.

---

1. Faber eventually converted to Roman Catholicism and began to write poetry that is distinctly Catholic. For that reason, some of his works must be read with caution.

apply

Jesus would often battle distraction and interruptions by withdrawing to quiet places for times of prayer. What habits have you instituted to hold distraction at bay when you pray? What habits should you institute that you haven't yet? Why is it better to pray badly (with distractions) than to not pray at all?

a prayer for God's presence and comfort

Friend of the Friendless: William Cowper

It is tremendously comforting to know that God always hears the Christian's prayers. Never does he turn his face away so that he cannot hear and never does he stop his ears so he will not listen. Never is he too distracted to pay attention and never is he too busy to give heed. No, our Father always hears our petitions. This gives us such confidence when we are sorrowful and afflicted, when we are downcast and suffering, for we know he is our Good Shepherd, our loving Father, our loyal Friend. When we cry to him, he will hear and he will act. There may be times when he answers with a loving no instead of an immediate yes. There may be times when he does not answer in the way we would like or at the time we would prefer. But there is never a time when we cry out to him in our need and he ignores us altogether. Because of the work of Christ on our behalf, we can have complete confidence that we are seen, known, and heard.

observe

William Cowper is known as one of the finest poets of the English language. He was also a hymn-writer who worked closely with John Newton and who contributed many fine selections to one of history's most important hymnals, *Olney Hymns*. Cowper suffered with mental illness throughout his life, and many of his poems are expressions of a mind in deep distress. Yet they are also expressions of a man whose ultimate hope was in the Lord and who knew where to turn in his anguish. The best known of his hymns is "There Is a Fountain," while the best known of his poems is "Light Shining out of Darkness," which contains the famous lines "God moves in a mysterious way, / His wonders to perform."

pray

God of my life, to Thee I call;
Afflicted, at Thy feet I fall;

When the great water-floods prevail,
Leave not my trembling heart to fail.

Friend of the friendless and the faint,
Where should I lodge my deep complaint?
Where but with Thee, whose open door
Invites the helpless and the poor?

Did ever mourner plead with Thee
And Thou refuse that mourner's plea?
Does not the word still fixed remain
That none shall seek Thy face in vain?

Fair is the lot that's cast for me;
I have an Advocate with Thee.
They whom the world caresses most
Have no such privilege to boast.

Poor though I am, despised, forgot,
Yet God, my God, forgets me not;
And he is safe, and must succeed,
For whom the Lord vouchsafes[1] to plead.

Then hear, O Lord, my humble cry
And bend on me Thy pitying eye.

---

1. Graciously grants.

To Thee their prayer Thy people make:
Hear us for our Redeemer's sake.

—William Cowper, "Friend of the Friendless"

reflect

Psalm 42; Luke 22:43.

apply

Do you believe that when you cry out to God in your most difficult times, he hears you? Think of a time when you have seen God answer you, perhaps in a time of great sadness and difficulty, as you thank the Lord that he does not forget you and hears your prayers.

a prayer for God's continued presence

Lord, I Have Wrestled: J. Sharp

There are times when God seems very near to us and times when he seems very distant. The reality, of course, is that God is always present and that we are always indwelled by the Holy Spirit. But sometimes we are very far from God's *felt* presence—from a sense of his love and nearness. This may happen when we have sinned and failed to confess or it may happen when we have not sinned but God means for us to better understand the joy of his presence and to cry out for it like a parched man cries out for water. Sometimes God means for us to wrestle in prayer through a long and difficult night of the soul before he answers that request and once again gives us that sense of his immediate presence. And so as Christians we learn to ask God to be always near, always present, and to always grant us the blessing of a sense of his love for us and nearness to us.

observe

The themes of wrestling with God throughout the night and not letting him go call to mind the story of Jacob wrestling with God in Genesis 32. Note how the poet appropriates elements of that story to relate his own experience.

pray

Lord, I have wrestled through the livelong night
Do not depart,
Nor leave me thus in sad and weary plight,
Broken in heart;
Where shall I turn, if Thou shouldst go away,
And leave me here in this cold world to stay?
I have no other help, no food, no light
No hand to guide,
The night is dark, my home is not in sight,
The path untried;
I dare not venture in the dark alone—
I cannot find my way, if Thou be gone.

I cannot yet discern Thee, as Thou art;
More let me see,
I cannot bear the thought that I must pass
Away from Thee:
I will not let Thee go, except Thou bless.
O, help me, Lord, in all my helplessness.

—J. Sharp, "Lord, I Have Wrestled"

reflect

Psalm 66:18; Genesis 32:22–26.

apply

Have you ever come to God in prayer with a sense that you have nowhere else to turn, no one else who can help you? How has the Lord met you in that place of helplessness? And in times when you have felt distant from God, what factors have seemed to play a role in that sense of separation? How did you respond?

a prayer for love and unity

One in Christ: Henry Van Dyke

The Bible knows nothing of Christians who live the Christian life alone—those who choose not to be part of a local church. Rather, it is clear that God means for us all to belong to Christ's body as it is made manifest in local churches. There are many blessings we receive from attaching ourselves to this body, not the least of which is having a community in which we can deliberately deploy the gifts God has given us while benefiting from the gifts God has given to others. Another great blessing is the blessing of sanctification, for we find that God does a great work within us as we attach ourselves to this community and attempt to live in unity with people who are very different from us. In this community we learn to repent and forgive, to give and receive, to bless and be blessed. We learn that the fervent prayer of every Christian must be that God would help us actively live out the truth that, in his eyes, we are one body made up of many members.

observe

Henry Van Dyke was an American author, poet, professor, and pastor who lived from 1852 to 1933. A man of many talents and accomplishments, he was, among other things, a professor of English at Princeton University and the American ambassador to the Netherlands. His most popular works were probably the Christmas stories "The Other Wise Man" and "The First Christmas Tree," along with the poem "Time Is." Apart from those works, he wrote many other poems, including one titled "One in Christ."

pray

No form of human framing,
No bond of outward might,
Can bind Thy Church together, Lord,
And all her flocks unite;
But, Jesus, Thou hast told us
How unity must be:
Thou art with God the Father one,
And we are one in Thee.

The mind that is in Jesus
Will guide us into truth,
The humble, open, joyful mind
Of ever-learning youth;
The heart that is in Jesus
Will lead us out of strife,
The giving and forgiving heart
That follows love in life.

Wherever men adore Thee,
Our souls with them would kneel;
Wherever men implore Thy help,
Their trouble we would feel;
And where men do Thy service,
Though knowing not Thy sign,
Our hand is with them in good work,
For they are also Thine.

Forgive us, Lord, the folly
That quarrels with Thy friends,
And draw us nearer to Thy heart
Where every discord ends;
Thou art the crown of manhood,
And Thou of God the Son;
O Master of our many lives,
In Thee our life is one.

—Henry Van Dyke, "One in Christ"

reflect

John 17:10–22; 1 Corinthians 12:12–13.

apply

As you reread the poem, what are some of the ways in which the poet sees us finding unity in Christ? Have you ever experienced unity in these ways with other believers? How is this different from a unity based on "human framing" or "outward might"? Would it be said of you that you labor toward the unity of your local church? In what ways are you failing to pursue and achieve unity with other Christians, and what might God be calling you to do about it?

a prayer of awe and worship

My God, How Wonderful Thou Art: F. W. Faber

The Bible describes two actions as complementary that we may think are contradictory. We are told to fear God and to love God. In fact, we cannot love God unless we first fear him. How is this possible? Because in this case "fear" means to revere or to honor—to properly assess and then to respond in a way that is appropriate. As we come to know God, we come to know him as a God who is holy, powerful, and wise, a God whose will cannot be interrupted or thwarted. We come to know him as a God who has the right to judge us according to the standard of his righteousness. Rightly, then, do we fear him! But then we also come to know him as a God who has made a way to be reconciled to us, a God who longs to have a relationship with us, and a God who loves to be loved by us. Rightly, then, do we fear him and love him. And rightly do we love him because we fear him.

observe

The poet uses the word "awful" in an antiquated form that perhaps we would do well to recover today. While we tend to define "awful" synonymously with "terrible" or "unpleasant," so that it speaks to a feeling of revulsion, Christians used to use it to speak of being filled with a sense of awe. Hence, Faber can write of "endless wisdom, boundless pow'r, and awful purity."

pray

My God, how wonderful Thou art,
Thy majesty how bright,
How beautiful Thy mercy seat,
In depths of burning light!

How dread are Thine eternal years,
O everlasting Lord;
By prostrate spirits, day and night,
Incessantly adored.

How wonderful, how beautiful,
The sight of Thee must be,
Thine endless wisdom, boundless pow'r,
And awful[1] purity.

O how I fear Thee, Living God,
With deepest, tend'rest fears,
And worship Thee with trembling hope,
And penitential tears.

Yet I may love Thee too, O Lord,
Almighty as Thou art;
For Thou hast stooped to ask of me
The love of my poor heart.

No earthly father loves like Thee,
No mother e'er so mild,
Bears and forbears, as Thou hast done
With me, Thy sinful child.

Father of Jesus, love's reward,
What rapture will it be,
Prostrate before Thy throne to lie,
And ever gaze on Thee!

—F. W. Faber, "My God, How Wonderful Thou Art"

1. Awe-inspiring.

reflect

Isaiah 6:1–7; Psalm 91:4.

apply

Notice that while the poet reflects on the awe-inspiring, fear-inducing beauty of God, he finds hope in the truth that God has invited us to love him. Do you ever find yourself marveling that God has stooped to ask of you the love of your poor heart? How does it change your understanding of God to know that he desires to be not merely obeyed by you but loved by you?

a prayer of submission to God

How Shall I Pray? Susan Coolidge

It is a question that most Christians wrestle with at one time or another: What is the point of praying? When God knows so much and we know so little, when God has complete knowledge of past, present, and future and we can barely see beyond the moment, when God has a will that is perfect and we have a will that is so terribly disordered, why would we pray? And how can we possibly pray with boldness—to "with confidence draw near to the throne of grace," as God commands (Heb. 4:16)? Who are we to prompt God in the way he should act? Yet the answer is as simple as this: God tells us to. God tells us to pray, and we must do as he says. Like the widow who has suffered injustice, we must pray with persistence; like the prophet who knew his sin, we must pray with humility; like the apostle who knew his need, we must pray continually. And like Jesus we must pray with confidence to the God who loves to hear our prayers and respond to them.

observe

The poet confesses that she does not fully know what to pray for or what to ask. She fears that her requests are "dim, short-sighted, ignorant," yet she still comes to ask. With this in mind, be sure to meditate on the request she makes in the final stanza.

pray

Father, how can I thus be bold to pray
That Thou shalt grant me that, or spare me this?
How should my ignorance not go astray,
How should my foolish lips not speak amiss,
And ask for woe, when fain[1] they would ask bliss?

How shall I dare to prompt Thee, the All-wise,
To show me kindness? Thou art ever kind.
What is my feeble craving in Thine eyes,

1. Gladly.

Which view the centuries vast, before, behind,
And sweep unnumbered worlds like
viewless wind?

Thy goodness ordereth what thing shall be,
Thy wisdom knoweth even my inmost want;
Why should I raise a needless prayer to Thee,
Or importune[2] Omnipotence to grant
My wishes, dim, short-sighted, ignorant?

And yet I come,—for Thou hast bidden
and said;
But not to weary Thee, or specify
A wish, but rather with this prayer instead:
"O Lord, Thou knowest,—give it or deny;
Fill up the cup of joy, or pass me by."

Just as Thou wilt is just what I would will.
Give me but this,—the heart to be content,
And, if my wish is thwarted, to lie still,
Waiting till puzzle and till pain are spent,
And the sweet thing made plain which the
Lord meant.

—Susan Coolidge, "How Shall I Pray?"

---

2. Beg or harass.

reflect

Hebrews 4:16; 1 Thessalonians 1:2.

apply

As the poet notes at the end, we may not always understand the Lord's will. And so she asks for a contented heart and patience to wait until the goodness of the Lord is evident and "till puzzle and till pain are spent." Have you ever felt that you did not know what to ask of the Lord? Or struggled with his answers to your prayers? Pray today with confidence, a mixture of boldness and humility, asking for a contented heart and patience in your puzzlement and pain.

a prayer that we would pray aright

Lord, When We Bend before Thy Throne: Joseph Dacre Carlyle

As you observe adherents of other faiths, you may notice how often they pray rote prayers—prayers that they repeat constantly but mindlessly. Such prayers may have been in the minds of Jesus' disciples when they asked him how to pray. And in his reply he did not tell them "pray this" and provide a specific prayer we are to mouth again and again; he said "pray *like* this" and offered a kind of model prayer. God expects us to pray thoughtfully, earnestly, and with hearts and minds fully engaged in the task. Yet we must admit there are times when we simply mouth words we do not mean—when we confess sins we do not intend to set aside, when we offer thanks for gifts we do not really want, and when we ask

God to grant character we do not intend to pursue. It does us good, then, to consider whether we are merely mouthing words that arise from a cold heart or pouring out words from hearts that are warmly eager to know God, to obey God, and to express love to God.

observe

Christians have long used written prayers, like the ones in this book (or the Book of Common Prayer or *The Valley of Vision*), to help them as they pray. While admitting that it is possible to merely mouth these as empty words, most Christians find that these written prayers help by offering fresh expressions of praise, gratitude, confession, and adoration to the Lord.

pray

Lord, when I bend before Thy throne,
And my confessions pour,
Teach me to feel the sins I own,
And hate what I deplore.

My broken spirit, pitying see;
True penitence impart;

And let a kindling[1] glance from Thee
Beam hope upon my heart.

When I disclose my wants in prayer,
May I my will resign;
And not a thought my bosom share
That is not wholly Thine.

Let faith each weak petition fill
And waft it to the skies,
And teach my heart 'tis goodness still
That grants it or denies.

—Joseph Dacre Carlyle, "Lord, When We Bend before Thy Throne"[2]

reflect

Psalm 34:18; Psalm 51:17.

apply

Do you sometimes find yourself prone to mouth empty prayers rather than heartfelt ones? Do you sometimes find

1. Inspiring, setting aflame.
2. Adapted from plural to singular.

yourself offering thanks or petitions that are insincere? What can you do about this? Take some time to admit to the Lord where your desires don't match his and your wants are not resigned to his will today. Ask for faith to trust in his unchanging goodness.

a prayer of praise to God for his justice and goodness

The Justice and Goodness of God: Benjamin Beddome

There are few descriptions of God superior to the one offered in the Westminster Shorter Catechism. "God is a spirit," it says, "infinite, eternal, and unchangeable in his being, wisdom, power, holiness, justice, goodness, and truth."[1] Among the attributes of God it lists two that may seem to be at odds: God is just and God is good. Yet these two are friends rather than enemies. When we say that God is just, we say that he is entirely righteous inside and

1. Westminster Shorter Catechism, answer 4.

out—upright in both his nature and his actions. When we say that God is good, we say that he is entirely pure inside and out—unblemished in his nature and his actions. God displays his goodness through his acts of justice. It is good of God to righteously punish those who defy him and it is good of God to righteously reward those who honor him. We do well to praise God for being good and we do well to praise God for being just, for it is through his justice—justice meted out against Christ on the cross—that we have been reconciled to him. And it is through his justice that we will, for all eternity, be able to praise him for his goodness.

observe

Observe the considerable list of attributes and actions for which the poet praises God—the attributes and actions that declare God's goodness and proclaim his justice. And then observe his response to them in the final stanza.

pray

Great God! my Maker and my King,
Of Thee I'll speak, of Thee I'll sing;
All Thou hast done, and all Thou dost,
Declare Thee good, proclaim Thee just.

Thy ancient thoughts and firm decrees;
Thy threatenings and Thy promises;
The joys of heaven, the pains of hell—
What angels taste, what devils feel;

Thy terrors and Thy acts of grace;
Thy threatening rod, and smiling face;
Thy wounding and Thy healing word;
A world undone, a world restored;

While these excite my fear and joy,
While these my tuneful lips employ,
Accept, O Lord, the humble song,
The tribute of a trembling tongue.

—Benjamin Beddome, "The Justice and Goodness of God"

reflect

Hebrews 6:10; Psalm 119:68.

apply

Note the juxtaposition of contraries throughout the poem—"Thy threatenings and Thy promises." Do you ever struggle to praise and thank the Lord for the good and the bad, for all that he has done? How does a biblical understanding of God's justice relate to his goodness and enable us to praise him for all that he is and does?

a prayer about the sufficiency of Christ

Complete in Him: James Edmeston

Christians have often considered what it means that we are "complete in him" (that is, in Christ) or, according to a slightly different interpretation, that we are "filled in him" (Col. 2:10). Regardless of the translation, the verse communicates a remarkable truth: because all power and authority has been given to Christ, and because he has chosen to share it with us, we have in him everything we need. We have been so closely united with him through the gospel that we do not need any saving apart from the salvation of Christ, we do not need any forgiveness other than the forgiveness he grants, we do not need any teaching apart from the teaching he gives through the Word. Through him we have all we need to be accepted by him, to be loyal to him, and to become like him. He is our sufficient Savior and we are complete and filled in him.

observe

James Edmeston was renowned as both an architect and a hymn-writer who is said to have written nearly two thousand hymns, the best known of which is "Lead Us, Heavenly Father, Lead Us." He had a special love for children, so he supported charities that cared for orphans while also writing simple hymns for younger singers. As an architect he designed a number of grand fountains and used that motif in some of his hymns and poems, including this one.

pray

Fountain of grace, rich, full, and free,
What need I, that is not in Thee?
Full pardon, strength to meet the day,
And peace which none can take away.

Doth sickness fill my heart with fear?
'Tis sweet to know that Thou art near;
Am I with dread of justice tried?
'Tis sweet to know that Christ hath died.

In life, Thy promises of aid
Forbid my heart to be afraid;

In death, peace gently veils the eyes;
Christ rose, and I shall surely rise.

O, all-sufficient Saviour, be
This all-sufficiency to me;
Nor pain, nor sin, nor death can harm
The weakest, shielded by Thine arm.

—James Edmeston, "Complete in Him"

reflect

Colossians 2:8–15; Ephesians 3:14–19.

apply

What does it mean to you that you are "in Christ" and are complete in him? Do you live like you are complete in Christ, like he is sufficient for all you need? Where, other than Christ, do you tend to turn for hope, help, or joy?

a prayer for humility

Jesus, Cast a Look on Me: John Berridge

There is no virtue more difficult to exemplify than humility. Though we are small, simple, and fallible creatures, we still think great thoughts of ourselves. We often put our desires ahead of other people's and our own will ahead of God's. We all need to learn humility, and there is no one better to learn it from than Jesus. Jesus expressed the greatest possible humility, for though he was God, though he had existed from all eternity, and though he was worthy of worship and praise, he chose to take on flesh and enter into this world. He chose to suffer all the ill effects of life in this world. He chose to be betrayed, beaten, and abandoned, then to suffer the wrath of God. In all of this he displayed supreme humility. No wonder, then, that "God has highly exalted him and bestowed on him the name that is above every name, so that at the name of Jesus every knee should bow, in heaven and on earth and under the earth, and every tongue confess that Jesus Christ is Lord, to the glory of God the Father" (Phil. 2:9–11).

observe

John Berridge was an Anglican minister who lived from 1716 to 1793. There was little fruit to the early years of his ministry, and he came to conclude that he was not a Christian. Upon turning to Christ in repentance and faith, he began to preach with power and was soon renowned for his proclamation of the gospel. He would later be commended by clergymen J. C. Ryle, Charles Spurgeon, and others as one of the great preachers of his era. He wrote many songs and poems that were eventually published as *Zion's Songs*.

pray

Jesus, cast a look on me;
Give me sweet simplicity,
Make me poor and keep me low,
Seeking only Thee to know;

All that feeds my busy pride,
Cast it evermore aside;
Bid my will to Thine submit;
Lay me humbly at Thy feet.

Make me like a little child,
Of my strength and wisdom spoiled,
Seeing only in Thy light,
Walking only in Thy might,

Leaning on Thy loving breast,
Where a weary soul may rest;
Feeling well the peace of God
Flowing from Thy precious Blood!

In this posture let me live,
And hosannas daily give;
In this temper let me die,
And hosannas ever cry!

—John Berridge,
"Jesus, Cast a Look on Me"

reflect

Philippians 2:5–11; James 4:6.

apply

The poet speaks of casting aside all that "feeds my busy pride." What would you say feeds your own pride? How might submitting your will to the Lord's, finding your rest in him, and seeking to know him help you resist pride? Do you find yourself growing in humility over the course of your Christian life? Consider asking someone you trust to tell you if you are a humble person. (You've got nothing to lose from asking the question!)

a prayer of grateful thanks

With Grateful Heart My Thanks I Bring: Poet Unknown

It is good to give thanks to the LORD, to sing praises to your name, O Most High" (Ps. 92:1). So said the psalmist centuries ago, and ever since all of God's people have replied with a hearty "Amen!" Giving thanks to God is our duty as beings who have been created by God and blessed to experience so many of his mercies. But giving thanks to God is not merely duty; it is also our great delight as beings who have been rescued by God and blessed to experience the evidences of his love, his care, and his saving grace. As God's just wrath fiercely falls upon those who will not honor God or give him thanks, so his blessings are upon those who do honor him and who do give him thanks for all of his works and ways (Rom. 1:21). When we pray, we rightly find our hearts making their petitions to God, but it is important as well that we pause to consider who God is and what he has done and allow our hearts to express the gratitude that God deserves.

observe

Over the years, Christians have written many poems and hymns that are adaptations of the biblical Psalms. This song is inspired by Psalm 138.

pray

With grateful heart my thanks I bring,
Before the great Your praise I sing;
I worship in Your holy place
And praise You for Your truth and grace;
For truth and grace together shine
In Your most holy word divine.

I cried to You, and You did save;
Your word of grace new courage gave;

The kings of earth shall thank You, Lord,
For they have heard Your wondrous word;
Yea, they shall come with songs of praise,
For great and glorious are Your ways.

O Lord, enthroned in glory bright,
You reign above in heav'nly height;
The proud in vain Your favor seek
But You have mercy for the meek;
Through trouble though my pathway be,
You will revive and strengthen me

You will stretch forth Your mighty arm
To save me when my foes alarm;
The work You have for me begun
Shall by Your grace be fully done;
Your mercy shall forever be;
O Lord, my Maker, think on me.

—Poet Unknown, "With Grateful
Heart My Thanks I Bring"

reflect

Romans 1:21; Psalm 92.

apply

Why is it important for us to express gratitude to God? How might beginning with thanksgiving shape and affect our prayers and requests? As you pray today and throughout this week, make every effort to begin with thanks. Are you as deliberate to consider what you should thank him for as you are to consider what to ask him for?

a prayer for the evening

God Who Madest Earth and Heaven: Reginald Heber

It is good to begin and end the day in prayer—to dedicate the day to the Lord as soon as we awaken and to thank him for it before we go to sleep. This gives us the chance to plead his help for the opportunities that will come and to seek his forgiveness for the ways we failed to embrace them. This gives us the opportunity to pray that he would guard us from temptation and to repent of any way we failed to take hold of his strength. And it gives us the opportunity to close each evening reflecting on the day that has just passed and asking God's blessing upon the one that will soon come. In this way we dedicate each day to his service and dedicate each night to resting so we can wake in the morning to serve him again. In this way we dedicate our lives to his service and reflect on the final night to come when we will close our eyes in death—and awake forever in his glorious presence.

observe

Observe the structure of the poem, how the opening lines of each stanza are quite long, how the middle lines are shorter, and how the final lines are shortest of all. Note how the poet is using the form of the poem to mimic the setting of the sun. He does this by visually creating lines that look like the sun setting in the sky and through lines that grow briefer—as if the one saying them is falling asleep.

pray

God, who made the earth and heaven,
    darkness and light:
You the day for work have given, for rest the night.
May Your angel guards defend me,
Slumber sweet Your mercy send me,
Holy dreams and hopes attend me
All through the night.

And when morn again shall call me to run
    life's way,

May I still, whate'er befall me, Your will obey.
From the pow'r of evil hide me,
In the narrow pathway guide me,
Never be Your smile denied me
All through the day.

Guard me waking, guard me sleeping, and,
when I die
May I in Your mighty keeping all peaceful lie.
When the last dread call shall wake me,
Then, O Lord, do not forsake me,
But to reign in glory take me
With You on high.

Holy Father, throned in heaven, all-holy Son,
Holy Spirit, freely given, blest Three in One:
Grant me grace, I now implore you,
Till I lay my crown before You
And in worthier strains adore You
While ages run.

—Reginald Heber, "God Who
Madest Earth and Heaven"[1]

1. Adapted from plural to singular.

reflect

1 Corinthians 15:13–19; Revelation 4:1–11.

apply

Are you in the habit of beginning each day in prayer? Are you in the habit of closing each day in prayer? While acknowledging that neither is explicitly commanded in Scripture, how might such a habit prove meaningful to you? If you do not have morning and evening prayers as a regular habit, consider adding them to your life this week, perhaps using some of the prayers of this book as a starting point.

a prayer of repentance

My Savior Whose Infinite Grace: Anna Waring

One of the unexpected realities of the Christian life is that the more we grow in God's grace, the more we understand how much more growth we still need. The more we grow in holiness, the more we understand how much sin remains. The more we come to appreciate God's amazing grace, the more we understand how undeserving we are. Yet this is not a cause for sorrow or despair, nor is it a reason to give up or turn back. Rather, it is a reason to praise God all the more, for it is proof that his Spirit is at work within us causing us to hate sin and love holiness. It provides the impetus to humbly plead with God that he would help us identify even more indwelling sin so we can earnestly put it to death. And it motivates us to continue confessing our sins and receiving his mercy. For the closer we come to meeting the Savior, the more we will want to be faithful imitators of our Savior.

observe

This poet displays gratitude to God for helping her see her faults. She displays humility by owning those sins and repenting of them. And she responds to this by praising God for his forgiving grace.

pray

My Savior whose infinite grace
Most kindly encompasses me,
Whose goodness more brightly I trace,
The more of my life that I see.—
The sins that I mournfully own,
Thy meekness and mercy exalt,—
And sweet is the voice from Thy throne,
That tenderly shows me a fault.

Even now, while my praises arise,
A sorrowful spirit is mine;
A spirit Thou wilt not despise,
For O! it is mourning with Thine.

My joy is in light from above,
The light which Thy kindness displays;
My grief is for lack of the love
That would tune my whole life to Thy praise.

My faithful Redeemer, forgive
The sin it has grieved Thee to see,
And let me remember to live
In the Spirit that glorifies Thee.
Though much in Thy child Thou hast borne,
Thy counsels still gently repeat,
And give me, if still I must mourn,
To mourn as a child at Thy feet.

—Anna Waring, "My Savior Whose Infinite Grace"

reflect

Psalm 51; Luke 7:36–50.

apply

Many followers of Christ have noted that as you grow in the Christian life, you find yourself becoming more aware of how much sin you've put to death as well as how much sin remains. Why do you think this is so? If that has been your experience, how do these twin realizations encourage you as you press on toward heaven?

a prayer to close the day

Evening Hymn: Mary Lundie Duncan

Sometimes the simplest of truths are the most sustaining of truths. Sometimes the simplest of songs are the ones that remain with us over the course of a lifetime. It is not unusual to hear that, in his last moments, a dying Christian has asked his gathered family to sing a song from his childhood, a song that provides the most basic explanation of the most essential truths. The best of us, after all, is but a little lamb before the great Shepherd, a creature that is feeble and defenseless and utterly dependent upon him. Though we can, should, and must grow in wisdom and maturity throughout the course of our lives, we still remain mere infants compared to our God and compared to who the Lord will make us when we reach his presence. Thus, whether we are closing out a day or closing out our lives, it is the simplest truths that so often serve us best, the simplest truths that fill our hearts and pass through our lips.

observe

This poet employs one of the Bible's simplest but sweetest metaphors to display the relationship of God to his people—that of a tender shepherd who cares for a helpless little lamb. None of us are so old, so strong, or so independent that we cannot benefit from considering how we are but little lambs in the care of our Good Shepherd.

pray

Jesus, tender Shepherd, hear me,
Bless Thy little lamb tonight;
Through the darkness be Thou near me.
Watch my sleep till morning light.

All this day Thy hand hath led me,
And I thank Thee for Thy care;
Thou hast clothed and warmed and fed me,
Listen to my evening prayer.

Let my sins be all forgiven,
Bless the friends I love so well;
Take me, when I die, to Heaven,
Happy there with Thee to dwell.

—Mary Lundie Duncan, "Evening Hymn"

reflect

Psalm 80:1; 1 Corinthians 14:20.

apply

What are some of the simple songs or poems that have best served you through your Christian life? What are some of the simplest truths that soothe your soul in times of pain, sorrow, or uncertainty?

a prayer for Christ's help

No Help in Self I Find: John Berridge

Many religions proclaim there is a deity of some kind, but in most cases this god is distant and unknowable, not the least bit interested in a relationship with mere human beings. One of the most precious and distinguishing features of the Christian faith is that it proclaims friendship between God and man. The Christian faith alone insists that God became man—that Jesus took on human nature without in any way diminishing his divine nature. As God he could represent God before man; as man he could represent man before God. He was in this way not only the perfect mediator but also both the Son of God and the friend of sinners. Shortly before he was crucified he said to his disciples (and by extension to us), "No longer do I call you servants, for the servant does not know what his master is doing; but I have called you friends, for all that I have heard from my Father I have made known to you"

(John 15:15). Through his suffering, death, and resurrection, Jesus reconciled us to the Father so we could have life and so we could have relationship—a sweet and beautiful friendship with God himself.

observe

There is value in allowing the poet to describe his own life through the epitaph he wrote for himself: "Here lies the remains of John Berridge, late Vicar of Everton, and an itinerate servant of Jesus Christ, who loved his Master and His work; and after running on His errands for many years, was caught up to wait on Him above. Reader! art thou born again? (No salvation without a new birth.) I was born in sin, February, 1716; remained ignorant of my fallen state till 1730; lived proudly on faith and works for salvation till 1754; was admitted to Everton Vicarage, 1755; fled to Jesus for refuge, 1755; fell asleep in Jesus, January 22, 1793."

pray

No help in self I find,
And yet have sought it well;
The native treasure of my mind
Is sin, and death, and hell.

To Christ for help I fly,
The Friend of sinners lost,
A refuge sweet, and sure and nigh,
And there is all my trust.

All other refuge fails,
And leaves my heart distrest;
But this eternally prevails,
To give a sinner rest.

Lord, grant me free access
Unto Thy piercèd side;
For there I seek my dwelling-place,
And there my guilt would hide.

—John Berridge, "No Help in Self I Find"

reflect

John 15:15; Matthew 9:10–13.

apply

Many of us have been taught the value of self-reliance, but in the first stanza we find the clear declaration: "No help in self

I find." Have you personally experienced this, the knowledge that you are not enough to meet your own needs? Perhaps you know intellectually that since you are a Christian, you are a friend of God's? Have you ever felt the beauty of this emotionally? What does it mean for you to be a friend of God and to know that he is a friend to you?

a prayer for mercy

Heal My Soul: Poet Unknown

There is much that God reveals to us about his nature, about who he is at his very heart. Few such attributes are more precious than this one: God is merciful. To be merciful is to treat others with compassion and to grant them forgiveness, and such divine mercy is one of the dominant themes of the Bible. It extends from Genesis to Revelation, from humanity's plunge into sin to God's full and final restoration in the future. It was mercy that kept God from immediately destroying Adam and Eve when they defied him, mercy that gave him patience with his people when they grumbled against him, mercy that caused him to deliver his people from their captivity in Babylon. And, of course, it was mercy that sent Jesus to the cross, for only an act of such grace and love could save us from our sins and reconcile us to God. Today it is mercy that compels God to continue to forgive us when we sin, to restore relationship when we have failed, and to press on in his work of making us into who he means for us to be. Rightly do we praise God for his sweet mercy!

observe

William Gadsby was an English clergyman who ministered in the nineteenth century. One of his contributions to the church was the compilation of a hymnal he called "A Selection of Hymns for Public Worship." This hymnal became widely used and included not only popular hymns by well-known writers but also a number of anonymous selections like this one.

pray

Lord, I approach Thy throne of grace,
Where mercy does abound,
Desiring mercy for my sin,
To heal my soul's deep wound.

O Lord, I need not to repeat
What I would humbly crave,
For Thou dost know, before I ask,
The thing that I would have.

Mercy, good Lord, mercy I ask;
This is the total sum;
For mercy, Lord, is all my suit;[1]
O let Thy mercy come.

—Poet Unknown, "Heal My Soul"

reflect

Exodus 34:6; Matthew 5:7.

apply

Note that the author speaks of mercy healing his soul's wound, as something he longs for and craves. What would drive someone to "crave" mercy in this way, and has that been a longing of your own soul? What does it mean to you that God is merciful, and how have you, personally, experienced the mercy of God?

1. Plea, request.

a prayer praising God for the Bible

How Precious, Lord, Thy Sacred Word: Isaac Watts

David stands alone in Scripture as receiving the accolade that he was a man after God's own heart (1 Sam. 13:14). Not surprisingly, then, he was also a man who loved God's Word. "Oh how I love your law!" he exclaimed. "It is my meditation all the day" (Ps. 119:97). "The law of the LORD is perfect," he said, and also sure, right, pure, true, righteous, sweet, and more to be desired than even the greatest riches (Ps. 19). It does us good to read his words and ask ourselves whether we love the Bible as much as he did. It does us good to ponder the fact that he knew only a small portion of the Scriptures when we have so much more and to consider whether we love God's complete revelation as much as David loved God's partial revelation. It does us good to consider what a treasure God has given us in his inerrant, complete, and sufficient Word.

observe

Isaac Watts (1674–1748), a renowned pastor and theologian, is also among the most notable of all Christian hymn-writers. As a man who popularized hymns and nudged the church away from singing exclusively psalms, he is often regarded as the father of English hymnody. He wrote nearly eight hundred hymns over the course of his life, many of which are still well known and much loved today. Among his most famous are "When I Survey the Wondrous Cross," "Joy to the World," and "Jesus Shall Reign Where'er the Sun." Besides writing hymns, he also published several volumes of poetry, much of it devotional in nature.

pray

How precious, Lord, Thy sacred Word,
What light and joy those leaves afford
To souls in deep distress!
Thy precepts guide my doubtful way,
Thy fear forbids my feet to stray,
Thy promise leads to rest.

Thy threat'nings wake my slum'bring eyes,
And warn me where my danger lies;
But 'tis Thy Gospel, Lord,
That makes the guilty conscience clean,
Converts the soul, and conquers sin,
And gives a free reward.

—Isaac Watts, "How Precious, Lord, Thy Sacred Word"[1]

reflect

Psalm 19; Psalm 119:97–104.

apply

What are some of the benefits of God's Word that Watts mentions here? Note in the final stanza how he describes the benefits of the gospel. Can you truly say that you love God's Word and attest to the "light and joy" the Bible afforded to you in your times of deep distress? If not, spend time reflecting on these benefits and ask the Lord to increase your love for his Word.

1. Adapted from plural to singular.

a prayer for the Spirit's power

Come, O Come, Thou Quick'ning Spirit: Heinrich Held (Translated by Charles W. Schaeffer)

It would be possible for God, in the very moment he saves our souls, to eradicate every last trace of the sin that dwells within us. Yet by his goodwill and for his good purposes, he has called us to instead wage a lifelong war against sin—to steadily and tenaciously "put to death . . . what is earthly" in us (Col. 3:5). We are to identify all that is evil, all that dishonors God, and all that expresses rebellion against him, to repent of it and put it to death. At the same time, we are also to learn what is good, to learn all that honors God and expresses conformity to him, and to bring it to life. This is the great task of every Christian! Yet even as we know this work will not be complete until the Lord calls us to himself, we can still be confident that it is possible to make great strides. How can we be so certain? Because God has given us the Holy Spirit for this very purpose—to dwell within us, to lead us to the truth, and to reshape us from the inside out.

observe

As you read the poem and pray it to the Lord, take special note of the various requests the author makes: for unfailing power, to seek that which pleases God, for God's knowledge to grow and spread, and much more.

pray

Come, O come, Thou quick'ning[1] Spirit,
God from all eternity!
May Thy power never fail me;
Dwell within me constantly.
Then shall truth and life and light
Banish all the gloom of night.

1. Life-giving.

Grant my heart in fullest measure
Wisdom, counsel, purity,
That I ever may be seeking
Only that which pleaseth Thee.
Let Thy knowledge spread and grow,
Working error's overthrow.

Show me, Lord, the path of blessing;
When I trespass on my way,
Cast, O Lord, my sins behind Thee
And be with me day by day.
Should I stray, O Lord, recall;
Work repentance when I fall.

Holy Spirit, strong and mighty,
Thou who makest all things new,
Make Thy work within me perfect
And the evil foe subdue.
Grant me weapons for the strife
And with vict'ry crown my life.

—Heinrich Held, "Come, O Come,
Thou Quick'ning Spirit"[2]

2. Adapted from plural to singular.

reflect

John 16:12–15; Colossians 3:5–17.

apply

As you note the various requests the author makes, consider some of the evidences of God's sanctifying grace that you have seen in your own life. Where have you seen the Holy Spirit changing and shaping you from within? Take some time to thank God for these evidences of his grace and answers to prayers.

a prayer for midday

Midday: George Doane

When he was in the most difficult of circumstances, David knew where to turn: "Evening and morning and at noon I utter my complaint and moan, and he hears my voice" (Ps. 55:17). He understood that in his sorrow he needed to be deeply reliant upon the Lord from the time he rose from bed to the time he returned. He knew that God was willing and eager to hear from him morning, noon, and night. He modeled a pattern of prayer that each of us ought to consider, whether we are in times of great sorrow or great joy. This is a pattern that begins the day by consecrating it to the Lord, pauses in the middle to praise God and seek his favor for the hours that remain, and then closes by confessing the sins of the day and seeking God's blessing through the night. In this way our whole lives can be marked by prayer and, through it, a humble reliance upon our God.

observe

The author seeks to give thanks to God and uses a threefold pattern that recognizes God as Maker, Preserver, and Savior. He concludes by noting that the source of this knowledge of God is his Word, praying that the Word might be as visible as the noonday sun.

pray

Father of lights, from Thee descends
Each good and perfect gift;
Then hear me while my thankful heart
In prayer of praise I lift:

I praise Thee, Maker, that Thou first
Didst form me from the clay,
And made my soul to love Thy name,
And worship, and obey.

I praise Thee, that the soul Thou gave,
Thou still in life dost hold—
Preserver, noon would fade to night,
Ere half Thy love were told!

I praise Thee, Saviour, that Thou didst

My soul from death release,
And, with Thine own atoning blood,
Procure me endless peace.

Maker, Preserver, Saviour, God!
What varied thanks I owe
To Thee, howe'er address'd, from whom
Such varied blessings flow.

To Thee, who on a darken'd world
Celestial light hast pour'd,
And told of heav'n, and taught the way,
In Thy most holy Word.

Wide as the blaze of noon is spread,
Spread Thou that word abroad:
I ask it, Saviour, in Thy name;
Maker, Preserver, God!

—George Doane, "Midday"[1]

reflect

1 Thessalonians 5:17; Luke 18:1–8.

---

1. Adapted from plural to singular.

apply

How do you honor God's Word where it instructs you to "pray without ceasing" (1 Thess. 5:17)? What patterns of prayer have you found most helpful in your life?

a prayer of confidence in God

Confident Pleading: Griffith Hugh Jones

When we are in times of great distress, often our minds can do little more than focus intently on the cause of our anguish. We find ourselves unable to pull our thoughts away from what we have lost or what we are being forced to endure. Though this may be understandable, there is a subtle danger that comes with it: we may be tempted to interpret God in light of our circumstances, to assume that since our circumstances are so painful, God must not be good or God must not be inclined toward us in love. What we need to do in our times of anguish is to turn our minds toward the Lord, to focus on who he is and what he has done, to remember his character, and to recount his deeds. It is then that we can interpret our circumstances properly, for we are interpreting them in light of the God who loves us, the God who has saved us, the God who has promised to bring us to his presence, and the God who promises he is working all things for the good of those who love him.

observe

This is a verse-by-verse meditation on the first eleven verses of Psalm 86. After reading it through a first time, consider reading Psalm 86 and then reading it through again.

pray

Bow down Thy ear, O Lord, and hear,
For I am poor and great my need;
Preserve my soul, for Thee I fear;
O God, Thy trusting servant heed.

O Lord, be merciful to me
For all the day to Thee I cry;
Rejoice Thy servant, for to Thee
I lift my soul, O Lord Most High.

For Thou, O Lord, art good and kind,
And ready to forgive Thou art;
Abundant mercy they shall find
Who call on Thee with all their heart.

O Lord, incline Thine ear to me,
My voice of supplication heed;
In trouble I will cry to Thee,
For Thou wilt answer when I plead.

There is not God but Thee alone,
Nor works like Thine, O Lord Most High;
All nations shall surround Thy throne
And their Creator glorify.

In all Thy deeds how great Thou art!
Thou one true God, Thy way make clear;
Teach me with undivided heart
To trust Thy truth, Thy name to fear.

—Griffith Hugh Jones, "Confident Pleading"

reflect

Romans 8:28; Ezra 8:22.

apply

When you are called to endure a time of great distress, how can you ensure you are interpreting your circumstances properly? How can you make sure you are focusing your thoughts on God rather than solely on your suffering? What Bible passages can guide you in this?

a prayer for the last days

Once More, O Lord, Thy Sign Shall Be: George Doane

When Jesus Christ took on flesh and came to this earth, he came in weakness—as a baby who was as helpless and as dependent upon his mother as you or I. When Jesus Christ lived on this earth, he lived in weakness—as a man who grew hungry and tired and who experienced sorrow and grief. When Jesus Christ died on this earth, he died in weakness—broken and abandoned upon a cross. But when Jesus Christ returns to this earth, there will be no sign of weakness, for "God has highly exalted him and bestowed on him the name that is above every name, so that at the name of Jesus every knee should bow, in heaven and on earth and under the earth, and every tongue confess that Jesus Christ is Lord, to the glory of God the Father" (Phil. 2:9–11). When he returns, it will be not in weakness but in strength, not in quietness but in power, not to bear our sin but to judge the sins of all the world. Best of all, he will return so we can live with him, reign with him, and live forever in his perfect presence.

observe

This poem employs strong and evocative language, much of it meant to capture the moment of Christ's return. Observe, though, how by the closing lines the tone changes from terrified to triumphant and from confronting to comforting.

pray

Once more, O Lord, Thy sign shall be
Upon the heavens display'd,
And earth and its inhabitants
Be terribly afraid:
For, not in weakness clad, Thou com'st,
My woes, my sins to bear,
But girt with all Thy Father's might,
His judgment to declare.

The terrors of that awful day
O who can understand?

Or who abide, when Thou in wrath
Shall lift Thy holy hand?
The earth shall quake, the sea shall roar,
The sun in heaven grow pale;
But Thou hast sworn, and wilt not change,
Thy faithful shall not fail.

Then grant me, Saviour, so to pass
My time in trembling here,
That when upon the clouds of heaven
Thy glory shall appear,
Uplifting high my joyful head,
In triumph I may rise,
And enter, with Thine angel train,
Thy palace in the skies.

—George Doane, "Once More,
O Lord, Thy Sign Shall Be"[1]

reflect

Philippians 2:9–11; 1 Thessalonians 4:16–18.

1. Adapted from plural to singular.

apply

How does the hope of Christ's returning to right all wrongs and renew all things give you hope to endure the challenges of today? Do you diligently pray for Christ's return? And do you diligently pray that you—and those you love—would be ready and waiting at that final hour?

a prayer to remain faithful to the end

O Jesus, I Have Promised: John Ernest Bode

It has long been the conviction of Christians that once we have truly come to Christ in repentance and faith, we can never fall away from that faith. Those who have been justified can never be unjustified; those who have been indwelled by the Spirit will never be abandoned by him. Yet Christians have also agreed that it is possible for us to deceive ourselves and to deceive other people into thinking we have trusted in Christ when we have not. Hence we are told to be diligent in confirming our "calling and election" (2 Peter 1:10). Knowing that we can be self-deceived, we must examine our lives to ensure we are living as Christians are called to live—that we are putting sin to death, coming alive to righteousness, and finding ever-greater joy in our relationship with the Lord Jesus Christ. And always we must pray that God would graciously preserve us by his Spirit so we can live in a way that is pleasing to him, then finish our race well and go to be with him forever.

observe

The poet begins by affirming that he has promised to serve Jesus to the end of his life. But he knows this will not be easy, for in the second stanza he provides a long list of the enemies and temptations that will challenge him for mastery of his life. This is why, in the third stanza, he pleads with God to give him what he needs to overcome those challenges. By the end he turns his heart away from what *he* has promised and toward what *Jesus* has promised—the ultimate affirmation that he will, indeed, remain faithful.

pray

O Jesus, I have promised
To serve Thee to the end;
Be Thou forever near me,
My Master and my Friend;
I shall not fear the battle

If Thou art by my side,
Nor wander from the pathway
If Thou wilt be my Guide.

O let me feel Thee near me,
The world is ever near;
I see the sights that dazzle,
The tempting sounds I hear;
My foes are ever near me,
Around me and within;
But, Jesus, draw Thou nearer,
And shield my soul from sin.

O let me hear Thee speaking
In accents clear and still,
Above the storms of passion,
The murmurs of self-will;
O speak to reassure me,
To hasten or control!
O speak, and make me listen,
Thou Guardian of my soul!

O Jesus, Thou hast promised
To all who follow Thee
That where Thou art in glory
There shall Thy servant be;
And, Jesus, I have promised

To serve Thee to the end;
O give me grace to follow,
My Master and my Friend!

—John Ernest Bode, "O Jesus, I Have Promised"

reflect

John 12:26; 2 Peter 1:5–11.

apply

Do you ever struggle with doubts about your salvation? Where do you turn for comfort when this happens? Instead of taking it for granted, it is good to take time today to pray to the Lord that, by his grace, you will persevere to the end. In addition to the encouragement of Scripture, it can be helpful to hear from others who might note evidence of grace in your life. Are there people who can speak into your life to tell you whether you are showing the marks of the Christian? If so, consider inviting their feedback today.

a prayer to listen and act

Lord, Speak to Me, That I May Speak: Frances R. Havergal

There are so many ways in which God blesses his people, in which he pours out upon us the riches that are ours in Christ. We come to learn that God blesses us for a specific purpose—he blesses us so we, in turn, can be a blessing to others. These riches of his grace are meant not to be held tight or selfishly hoarded but joyfully dispensed to others. We pray that we would come to better understand God's Word so we might help others better understand it; we pray that God would give us spiritual or physical strength so that we might be able to support those who are weak and faltering; we pray that God would grant us a greater love for him so that this love might overflow in service to others. God gives us these gifts so that we ourselves might have the blessing of being a gift to our brothers and sisters in Christ.

observe

Observe how Havergal provides a long list of verbs—sometimes one in a stanza and sometimes two: *speak*, *seek*, *lead*, *feed*, *stand*, *stretch*, and so on. These verbs are the key to her poem and key to the kind of service she wishes to render to others.

pray

Lord, speak to me, that I may speak
In living echoes of Thy tone;
As Thou has sought, so let me seek
Thine erring children lost and lone.

Oh, lead me, Lord, that I may lead
The wand'ring and the wav'ring feet;
Oh, feed me, Lord, that I may feed
Thy hung'ring ones with manna sweet.

Oh, strengthen me, that while I stand
Firm on the rock, and strong in Thee,
I may stretch out a loving hand
To wrestlers with the troubled sea.

Oh, teach me, Lord, that I may teach

The precious things Thou dost impart;
And wing my words, that they may reach
The hidden depths of many a heart.

Oh, give Thine own sweet rest to me,
That I may speak with soothing pow'r
A word in season, as from Thee,
To weary ones in needful hour.

Oh, fill me with Thy fullness, Lord,
Until my very heart o'erflow
In kindling thought and glowing word,
Thy love to tell, Thy praise to show.

Oh, use me, Lord, use even me,
Just as Thou wilt, and when, and where,
Until Thy blessed face I see,
Thy rest, Thy joy, Thy glory share.

—Frances R. Havergal,
"Lord, Speak to Me,
That I May Speak"

reflect

1 Peter 4:10–11; 1 Corinthians 4:7.

apply

In what ways has God gifted you to be a blessing to others? How are you faithfully exercising your God-given gifts in service to other Christians, and especially within your local church? Are there any new ways God might be calling you to serve?

a prayer of praise to the triune God

Glory Be to God on High: Charles Wesley

There are times when we are so overwhelmed with the goodness of God and the wonder of being in relationship with him that we cannot help but praise his name. There are times when we consider who God is and our mouths cannot stay silent, our eyes cannot stay dry. There are times when we consider what God has done and our hands cannot help but rise, our knees cannot help but bow. In these times we feel the reality of what Jesus said when some questioned whether it was right to praise him: "I tell you, if these were silent, the very stones would cry out" (Luke 19:40). Or we think of Isaiah proclaiming that before God even the mountains and hills will break forth into singing and the trees of the field clap their hands in joy (Isa. 55:12). In these times we must cry out from the heart, cry out in joy and wonder, "Glory be to God on high!"

observe

Few hymn-writers have left a greater legacy than Charles Wesley. Wesley, along with his brother John and their mutual friend George Whitefield, were cofounders of the movement that became known as Methodism. This was a movement that highly valued songs, and Charles became its most prolific hymn-writer, writing more than six thousand over the course of his life. These included the perennial favorites "O for a Thousand Tongues," "Christ the Lord Is Risen Today," and "Hark! The Herald Angels Sing." Besides writing hymns, he also penned many poems, though often the line between the two was blurry. In either form, he was particularly adept at describing the experience of conversion, as in "And Can It Be": "Long my imprison'd Spirit lay, / Fast bound in sin and nature's Night: / Thine eye diffus'd a quick'ning ray; / I woke; the dungeon flam'd with light; / My chains fell off, my heart was free, / I rose, went forth, and follow'd Thee."

pray

Glory be to God on high,
God whose glory fills the sky;
Peace on earth, and man forgiven,
Man, the well-beloved of Heaven.

Hail, by all Thy works adored!

Hail, the everlasting Lord!
All Thy glories I confess,
Infinite and numberless.

Holy Spirit, Thee I own;
Thee, O Christ, the only Son!
Lamb of God for sinners slain,
Saviour of offending men.

Praise the name of God Most High;
Praise Him, all below the sky;
Praise Him, all ye heav'nly host,
Father, Son, and Holy Ghost.

—Charles Wesley, "Glory Be to God on High"

reflect

Isaiah 55:10–13; Psalm 148.

apply

In what situations do you most feel the longing to praise and glorify God? How, over the course of your Christian life, has your growth in the knowledge of God fueled your love of worshiping God?

a prayer for blessing in our troubles

To a Friend in Deep Affliction: A. M. Hull

It is one of the most difficult lessons that every Christian must learn: some of God's richest blessings come only through the deepest pains. Just as we cannot see the stars until the sun has set and darkness has fallen, we cannot know some of God's choicest blessings until we have come into a time of trial. This is not to say we should seek out trials or plead with God for them to come upon us—we should not wish evil upon ourselves or anyone else. But it does mean that when God's providence decrees a time of suffering, we can expect that God will sanctify it for his purposes by teaching us precious truths we would otherwise not have come to know, by causing us to depend more upon him in prayer, by motivating us to rely more deeply on his promises, and by having us long even more to be in his presence. And so in our suffering we do well to pray for relief, but we also pray, with Christ, "Nevertheless, not as I will, but as you will" (Matt. 26:39).

observe

Observe how the poet interprets this time of suffering. She professes the sovereignty of God in it and does not deny that even though it is very difficult, it is in some way his will. She then describes what God so often accomplishes in times of sorrow—he provides a sense of his love, a knowledge of his ways, new reasons to praise his name. And then she submits to God in the suffering, knowing that God has his purposes and that, because of his love, those purposes must be good.

pray

Lord, dost Thou give the painful wound?
And shall I turn away?
Nay, rather for the sorest stroke
The trusting heart would stay.

For faithful are Thy kindly wounds,
Though 'neath the bruise we bend;

Sweet is the secret of Thy love,
Unfolded in the end.

They deepen in our fickle hearts
The knowledge of Thy ways;
They put new songs within our lips,
And give new themes of praise.

And when Thy chastening is past,
More gladness far is ours,
Than when the sweets of earthly joy
Increased on us in showers.

Then do for me, O blessèd Lord,
Whate'er Thou thinkest well;
Let sorrow sound upon my soul
Its deep, its dismal knell,[1]

If but the music of Thy love
With soft, yet deeper tone,
Awakes the soul to find in Thee
Delights before unknown.

—A. M. Hull, "To a Friend in Deep Affliction"[2]

---

1. The sound of a bell.
2. Partially adapted from plural to singular.

reflect

Matthew 26:39; Ecclesiastes 8:12.

apply

The poet speaks of a deeper experience of delight in God through pain. In the past, have you been able, in your times of sorrow, to submit them to God and wait for him to work through them? How have you seen God increase your love and joy following times of suffering?

a prayer for God's presence

Far from My Thoughts, Vain World, Begone: Isaac Watts

There are times when our hearts are eager to be with the Lord, when they prove to be especially receptive to his Word. But there are also times when our hearts are not at all eager to be with the Lord, when they prove especially uninterested in his Word or even hostile to it. We learn that if we wish to experience spiritual joy and warmth, if we wish to enjoy God's presence and be transformed by his Word, we must seek his help and favor. We must ask him to help us be disciplined in turning ourselves away from the world and its many trite distractions. We must plead with him to help us dutifully and patiently wait upon him, hear from him, enjoy him, and be touched by him. We must pray that he would give us holy desires and holy longings that would find their fulfillment in a sweet, real, and living relationship with him.

observe

Observe how the poet begins by speaking to himself and to his own soul, just as David sometimes did in the Psalms. But then notice how quickly he stops speaking to himself and begins speaking to Jesus. We would do well to learn from him.

pray

Far from my thoughts, vain world, begone,
Let my religious hours alone:
Fain would my eyes my Savior see;
I wait a visit, Lord, from Thee.

My heart grows warm with holy fire,
And kindles with a pure desire:
Come, my dear Jesus, from above,
And feed my soul with heavenly love.

The trees of life immortal stand
In fragrant rows at Thy right hand;
And in sweet murmurs, by their side,
Rivers of bliss perpetual glide.

Haste, then, but with a smiling face,
And spread the table of Thy grace;
Bring down a taste of fruit divine,
And cheer my heart with sacred wine.

Blest Jesus, what delicious fare!
How sweet Thy entertainments are!
Never did angels taste above
Redeeming grace, and dying love.

Hail, great Immanuel, all divine!
In Thee Thy Father's glories shine;
Thou brightest, sweetest, fairest one,
That eyes have seen or angels known.

—Isaac Watts, "Far from My Thoughts, Vain World, Begone"

reflect

Psalm 19; Psalm 73:25–26.

apply

What does your heart feast upon? What do you feed your desires? What do you seek to fulfill those longings? This is what will form and shape your spiritual taste buds. Are you in the habit of praying that God would stir your heart with longing for him? Do you plead that he would give you a longing to set aside distractions and lesser affections so you can be spiritually fed and nourished by him?

a prayer to be unashamed of Jesus

Ashamed of Jesus: Joseph Grigg

God's patience toward his people is displayed in a host of ways, but perhaps in this more than any other: he continues to love us even when we are ashamed of him. And what Christian can't think of a time—or even many times—when we have been ashamed to admit that we are followers of Christ or when we have been ashamed to take a ready opportunity to tell others about Christ? What Christian has never at times felt that it is shameful to be associated with Jesus or associated with the people he loves and died for? Yet we must repent of this shame and instead be willing to boldly profess the name of Jesus and proclaim the gospel of Jesus, pondering soberly what Jesus said, "Whoever denies me before men, I also will deny before my Father who is in heaven" (Matt. 10:33). God is good to forgive us for our shame and good to grant us the grace to proclaim before all the world that Jesus is Lord.

observe

The best poems often have a kind of continuity between the first stanza and the last, in which a theme from the beginning returns at the end. Note how in the first stanza of this poem a man considers being ashamed of Jesus and how in the final stanza he rejoices that Jesus is not ashamed of him.

pray

Jesus, and shall it ever be,
A mortal man ashamed of Thee?
Ashamed of Thee, whom angels praise,
Whose glories shine through endless days?

Ashamed of Jesus! sooner far
Let evening blush to own a star;
He sheds the beams of light divine
O'er this benighted soul of mine.

Ashamed of Jesus! just as soon
Let midnight be ashamed of noon;
'Tis midnight with my soul, till He,
Bright Morning Star, bid darkness flee.

Ashamed of Jesus! that dear friend
On whom my hopes of bliss depend?
No; when I blush be this my shame,
That I no more revere His name.

Ashamed of Jesus! yes, I may,
When I've no guilt to wash away,
No tear to wipe, no good to crave,
No fears to quell, no soul to save.

Till then—nor is my boasting vain—
Till then I boast a Saviour slain;
And, oh, may this my glory be,
That Christ is not ashamed of me!

—Joseph Grigg, "Ashamed of Jesus"

reflect

Matthew 10:26–33; 2 Timothy 2:8–13.

apply

What are some situations in which you might find yourself ashamed of Jesus (or of his words and teachings)? In what direction does the author point us to train our hearts to move from feeling shame to boasting in Christ instead?

a prayer to Jesus

Hymn: Poet Unknown

We can talk to God. This comes as no surprise, of course, since this entire collection of poetry has been about talking to God. But as it comes to its end and its final prayer, it would do us well to consider one more time the tremendous privilege it is to be able to talk to God. There are many people who speak to pieces of wood or stone and think they are talking to God. There are many people who speak into the night skies and hope fate will respond or the universe will hear. There are many who refuse to admit any notion of a power higher and holier than themselves. But we know that God is true and real, that God is merciful and gracious, and that God is willing and eager to hear us when we speak to him. We know he loves to hear from those who are his just as a father loves to hear from his son; he loves to care for those who are his as a mother loves to care for her daughter. And so we can speak to God confident that this gives him great delight. We can talk to God!

observe

Consider the poet's exalted descriptions of God: the one to whom all power is given, the one who reigns as the world's sovereign, the one whom angels obey, the one who sustains the earth and all that is in it. Then consider that this God invites us to speak to him and to make our sins, fears, and requests known to him. What a God we serve!

pray

Thou to whom all power is given,
Here on earth, above, in heaven,
Jesus, Saviour, mighty Lord,
Be Thy holy name adored!

In our hearts all-sovereign reign;
All the world be Thy domain!
May redeemed man, we pray Thee,
Like the angelic host, obey Thee.

Thou who dost the ravens feed,
Grant us all our bodies need;
Thou in whom we move and live
Daily grace sustaining give!

Pardon us, our sins confessing
Keep us from afresh transgressing;
May we pardon one another,
As becomes a sinning brother.

In temptation's dreadful hour,
Shield us with Thy gracious power.
From Satan's wiles our hearts defend,
Saviour, Comforter, and Friend!

Glory to Thee on earth be given,
Christ our King, the Lord of heaven;
Glory to Thee, great "First and Last,"
When this earth, and time, are past!

—Poet Unknown, "Hymn"

reflect

Matthew 28:18; 2 Peter 2:9.

apply

In what ways has this collection of prayers proven helpful to you? What are some of the next steps you might take as you press on in the life of a praying Christian?

conclusion

It is my hope that as you have read this book, you have come to a deeper appreciation of both prayer and poetry. And, of course, I hope you have come to appreciate the confluence of the two in prayers that are set to poetry.

Now that you have arrived at the end of this collection, I would encourage you to return to the poems and continue to pray them. Speaking personally, I have long since integrated them into my time of daily devotion. I pray one of these poems each day and have found that the more I pray them, the more I come to understand and treasure them. The more I understand and treasure them, the more they give voice to the cries of my heart.

I hope you will find, as I have, that there is blessing to be had in praying poetically—in praying the works of poetry our forebears in Christ have bequeathed to us. May their words become your words, and their prayers your prayers.

index of poets and poems

Seasons of Sorrow

Tim Challies

An honest look at grief and fears, faith and hope. Combining personal narrative, sound theology, and beautiful writing, this is a book for anyone who has loved and lost.

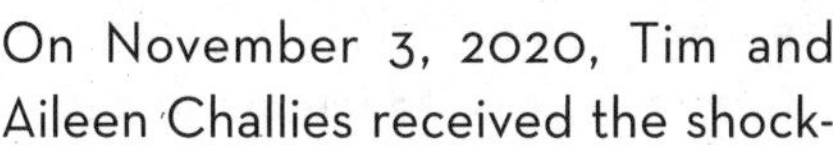
On November 3, 2020, Tim and Aileen Challies received the shocking news that their son Nick had died. A twenty-year-old student at the Southern Baptist Theological Seminary in Louisville, Kentucky, he had been participating in a school activity with his fiancée, sister, and friends when he became unconscious and collapsed.

Neither students nor a passing doctor nor paramedics were able to revive him. His parents received the news at their home in Toronto and immediately departed for Louisville to be together as a family. While on the plane, Tim, an author and blogger, began to process his loss through writing.

In *Seasons of Sorrow*, Tim shares real-time reflections from the first year of grief—through the seasons from fall to summer—introducing readers to what he describes as the "ministry of sorrow."

A Visual Theology Guide to the Bible

Tim Challies and Josh Byers

The deepest truths of the Bible made accessible so that they can be seen, understood, and experienced like never before, combining graphics and text to teach the nature and contents of the Bible in a fresh and exciting way.

For a beautiful, approachable, informative presentation of the concepts and principles of Scripture, turn to any page of *A Visual Theology Guide to the Bible* and be instantly immersed in the visuals and teachings of God's Word.

A Visual Theology Guide to the Bible is not only a wonderful introduction to the Christian life, it is a functioning guide for understanding and living out your faith.

You'll see how the Bible is put together, why the authors wrote each book, and what all of it means for your life today. What's more, you'll learn why the Bible can be trusted and how to answer common criticisms of the Bible.

Used in conjunction with Tim Challies and Josh Byers' bestselling book, *Visual Theology*, this unique resource helps you connect the truth of the Bible to your life, showing how God's eternal truth leads to transformation.

Visual Theology

Tim Challies and Josh Byers

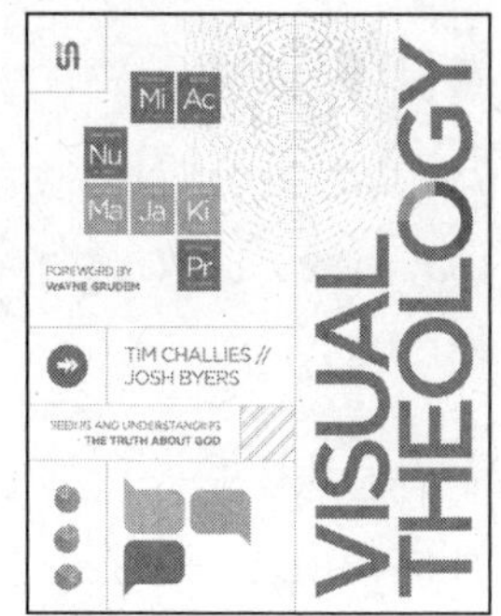

A visual introduction to systematic theology

We live in a visual culture, increasingly relying on infographics and other visuals to help us understand new and difficult concepts. But the visual portrayal of truth is not a novel idea. God himself communicated his truth visually though the tabernacle, the sacraments, and even the cross.

In *Visual Theology*, Tim Challies and Josh Byers use a combination of words and illustrations to convey the concepts and principles of systematic theology in a fresh, beautiful, and informative way. They have made the deepest truths of the Bible accessible in a way that can be seen and understood by a visual generation, focusing on four foundational disciplines:

- Growing close to Christ
- Understanding the work of Christ
- Becoming like Christ
- Living for Christ

This unique resource is an inviting and artful way to learn theology, comprehend difficult Bible concepts, and grow in your faith.

Epic

An Around-the-World Journey through Christian History

Tim Challies

Thirty-three fascinating objects. One amazing story.

Join author and pastor Tim Challies as he embarks on a three-year journey spanning multiple continents and some of the most unusual places in the world. Tim introduces you to thirty-three carefully selected objects that help you understand the long and complicated history of Christianity in a unique and creative way.

Beginning with Jesus and the early church, Challies looks at:

- The importance of graffiti on an ancient jail cell
- The creedal significance of a carving on a museum statue
- The enduring importance of ancient manuscripts and books
- And much more!

Along the way, you'll discover the story you're already a part of. Features:

- An epic journey: 24 countries, six continents, 75 flights, 80 museums
- Beautiful full-color book design featuring the objects and Tim's journey
- The complete experience: a ten-episode documentary is also available, taking you on location and providing an immersive experience for understanding the history of Christianity.